Be Challenged

Be Challenged

by

Warren W. Wiersbe

MOODY PRESS

CHICAGO

Revised Edition
Former title: *Be a Real Teen*

All Scripture quotations, unless noted otherwise, are from the *New American Standard Bible*, © 1960, 1962, 1963, 1968, 1971, 1972, 1973, 1975, and 1977 by The Lockman Foundation, and are used by permission.

The material in chapters 4 and 8 appeared in a different form in *Moody Monthly*; and the material in chapter 6 also appeared in a different form in *Youth for Christ* magazine. I appreciate the willingness of the editors of these two publications to allow me to use this material in this book.

Library of Congress Cataloging in Publication Data

Wiersbe, Warren W.
Be challenged.

 Summary: Principles derived from Biblical teachings and exemplified by the lives of Biblical characters are applied to the realities of modern life.

 1. Youth—Religious life. 2. Bible—Biography.
Juvenile literature. [1. Christian life. 2. Bible]
I. Title.
BV4531.2.W523 1982   248.8'3   82-12404
ISBN 0-8024-1080-4

4 5 6 Printing/LC/Year 87 86

Printed in the United States of America

Acknowledgment

The author would like to express appreciation to Miriam Levengood for her excellent editorial help.

Contents

Preface

THIS BOOK IS for teenagers (and adults who want to help teenagers), but it contains some dangerous ideas.

The first is that today's young people are caught in a deadly conspiracy that could rob them of their adult happiness as well as their enjoyment of their teen years.

The second is that today's young people don't need sugarcoated advice from TV or music idols; they need down-to-earth principles from real young people. This book contains principles, not fancy slogans or bits of adult advice.

The third is that the best place to find those principles is in the Bible. Be prepared for a lot of Bible reading as you meet six Bible teenagers and learn the principles that guided them to success. Frankly, I find that the Bible is the most exciting, practical Book in the world! And the teenagers of the Bible are the most wonderful young people in the world!

Those ideas may not be new. I've been sharing them with thousands of young people and adults in youth conferences and seminars for the past several years, so I know they work.

I hope you'll let them work in your life.

WARREN WIERSBE

1

Wanted:
Real Teenagers!

IT MAY BE bad psychology, but I'm going to begin this book with a warning. It's this: *there is a plot afoot to change you into an artificial adult instead of a real teenager.* There are subtle forces at work in your world that could rob you of the greatest thrill of your seven teen years—the thrill of just being yourself, of following the pattern God set for you, and of emerging someday into the adult world, ready for life.

After all, if you aren't a real teenager today, how can you ever be a real adult tomorrow? If you're living on substitutes now, how will you ever recognize and enjoy the real values of life when they come your way?

In many respects today's young people are

victims of mistakes that some adults have made, mistakes that society has picked up and promoted and about which you and I can do very little. But one thing you can do is recognize the forces that are at work, identify them, and learn to overcome them.

Before we talk about those forces, however, let's try to discover what a real teenager is.

I think the first characteristic of a real teenager is that *he has accepted himself*. He isn't trying to be a child (although there will be times when he'll act like a child); neither is he trying to be an adult. He has looked at himself in the mirror and said, "Friend, you are a teenager! This means seven years ahead of you when you'll be misunderstood, pushed, criticized, and perhaps even rejected. But you'll also be taught, loved, encouraged, and helped in many ways to become a balanced adult. Now, stick with the job of being yourself; grow up while you grow old, and discover the things that really count."

Too many young people these days celebrate their thirteenth birthdays by jumping headlong into adult activities and privileges for which they simply aren't prepared. "I'm a teenager now, Mom. Can't I go steady?" Instead of accepting their teen years as a time of transition, a bridge between the dependence of childhood and the interdependence of adulthood, they immediately dive off the bridge into the river of life—and find themselves drowning in demands that are over their heads.

This is why so many young people develop emotional problems, create difficulties at home, and worse yet, get into trouble with the law. They're plugging their 6-volt toys into a 220-volt generator and blowing all their fuses before they really have a chance to live.

A real teenager, then, accepts the fact that he *is* a teenager, and that his main task in life is learning how to be an adult. He accepts himself, his strengths and weaknesses, his world around him, and the challenge God has placed in his hands. He's willing to wait for adult privileges. The rest of his crowd may run ahead, sneering as they pass him on the road of life; but the real teenager knows he'll catch up with them in a few years and find them bored with life, their dynamic all gone, while he's ready to move into the challenges of adulthood.

So, make up your mind right now that you're going to be a *real teenager*—not an artificial adult, not an actor, not a pretender. Make up your mind that you're going to *invest* in these teen years, and not just "spend them," knowing that your investments will pay big dividends in the years to come.

Now, don't get the idea that a real teenager sits on the sidelines and watches everybody else have the fun! Quite the contrary is true. The teenager who knows who he is, what he's supposed to do, and where he's going will always get more out of life than the "artificial adult" who is trying to be something God never meant him to be. After all, little Josephine can put mother's high heels on her little five-year-old feet, and wrap mother's best dress around her five-year-old body, but that won't make her an adult. She'll discover, instead, that the shoes keep her from making any progress and the dress has a way of making her fall. Transfer that scene to your high school campus and you'll understand why some of your "grown-up" friends never seem to get anywhere and are usually falling into trouble.

No, the real teenager enjoys life a lot more than the teens who want to enjoy adult privileges before they're ready to accept adult responsibilities. The real teenager has that sense of stability that gives him poise and purpose, and that rescues him from embarrassing and even dangerous situations.

Something else is true of a real teenager: he not only accepts himself, but *he understands himself*. He realizes that important changes are going on in his body, his home, and his world. Those changes don't frighten or perplex him because he understands where they came from and what the final results will be. Ignorance always leads to insecurity, but understanding leads to strength and stability.

Here is where the "artificial adult" suffers: he

plunges into adult experiences without being able to handle them, and without really understanding all that's involved. Those experiences become destructive instead of creative in his life, and he ends up in worse shape than when he started! Jesus said, "And you shall know the truth, and the truth shall make you free" (John 8:32). But they ignore the truth, and the result is bondage.

A third characteristic of the real teenager is that *he lives with a serious purpose in mind.* He realizes that he must *employ* his teen years and not simply *enjoy* them; that he has a job to do during these seven important years, *a job that can be done at no other time in life.* If Johnny fails to learn some good habits while still at home, we hope the kindergarten teacher will straighten things out. Grade school problems can sometimes be solved in junior high school. But if you let your teen years slip through your fingers, you'll take into your adult life the weaknesses and problems that can be magnified and multiplied into adult failures. The old adage bears repeating: "What you are going to be, you are becoming right now."

A real teenager, then, accepts himself, understands himself, and directs himself by a serious purpose. There is one final characteristic: *a real teenager knows that he can't do the job alone.* You'll never hear him shout, "Leave me alone! I can run my own life!" He knows better. He knows that he needs his family, his friends, and his God if he's going to make a success of his teen years. He realizes that he'll have to follow the best possible examples, listen to the best possible counsel, and aim for the best possible goals.

That's why I've written this book. I want to share with you some basic principles that can make your teen years a thrilling success instead of a tragic failure—principles that deal with the down-to-earth affairs of your life. I want to introduce you to six teenagers from the Bible— *real teenagers*—and show you from their successes and failures how you can be a real teenager.

I have been living with these Bible teens for years now, and I want you to know them and learn the secrets that made them great. I want you to meet Joseph and let him tell you how you can make your dreams come true. I want David to explain how to prepare for a fantastic future. (After all, David started as a shepherd and ended up a king!) Daniel will share with you the secret of being a transformer instead of a conformer; and Mary will tell you how to have real dynamic in your life. I want Timothy to explain what it means to be diligent and get the job done; and finally, I want you to meet the Ideal Teenager, Jesus Christ, who will show you the perfect example of what a teenager ought to be.

But first, I promised to explain the forces at work in your world that are trying to rob you of your important teen years. Before you turn the page, tell yourself and God that, with His help, you're going to be, not an "artificial adult," but a real teenager.

2

Somebody's After You

PLEASE DON'T GET the idea that an adult mastermind in some hidden office is plotting the downfall of the American youth. It really isn't that bad. But you had better recognize the fact that there are definite forces at work in your world, trying to rob you of your teen years. You and I may not be able to reform them, but at least we can learn to recognize and resist them.

All this fuss over American young people dates back to 1945, a post-war era when for the first time teenagers moved into the spotlight. Of course, the war itself helped to bring this about. Thousands of teenage boys were in uniform, and thousands more were helping the war effort at home. With millions of men away from home in the armed forces, the teens back home were on top of the population totem pole. They were Very Important People! Boys had to do men's work, so why shouldn't the boys be treated like men?

Another factor was the rise of juvenile delinquency. Nobody is quite sure what brought about the increase in teenage crime, but one thing is sure: it put the teenager on the front page of every American newspaper, and the public had to sit up and take notice. In fact, it almost came to the place where adults thought that "delinquent" and "teenager" were synonymous words! The end result was that people began to notice the younger generation and even began to be afraid of them!

The population explosion helped, too. From 1945 to the present, the world has seen an increase in population that has definitely affected every area of life. Big families became popular after World War II, and those new babies eventually became teenagers.

Now, when a segment of the population begins to increase in size, get involved in serious problems, and raise new questions, the adults have to sit up and take notice. So, shortly after the war, people began to study the American teenager. Purdue University set up its "Public Opinion Poll" that resulted in the studies found in the book *The American Teen-ager*. Mr. Eugene Gilbert established his Gilbert Youth Survey organization and began telling the American public (through his newspaper column) what songs teens liked, what they ate, how they spent their leisure time, and what they felt should be done about the world situation. The field of adolescent psychology suddenly became important, and experts on teens began writing books for teachers, parents, and the teens themselves.

All of this led to a great opportunity for somebody to make a lot of money. After all, if you have millions of teenagers, you also have millions of customers. And if those teens are starting to feel important in the world, why not assist them by treating them like adult customers? It was here that Big Business moved in, assisted by Big Advertising, and began their "artificial adult" propaganda that is ruining millions of young people today.

Here's how it works. Teens have money, and that money has to be spent. The smart thing to do is to create a market. The result? Teen fashions, teen music, teen magazines, teen idols, and a vast array of items that today's teens think they cannot live without. The manufacturer knows that American young people spend billions of dollars a year, and he wants to get his fair slice of the watermelon. He knows that a steady teen customer is sure to become a steady adult customer, so his promotion to teens is a lifetime investment.

I believe that *Seventeen* was the first teenage magazine to come out into mass circulation, and it was devoted primarily to helping girls become "mature teens." It was soon followed by a parade of teen magazines catering to the adolescent reader and most of those now revolve around teen idols, rock music, dating advice, self-help articles, and general news and views of the teenage world. Some of them are close to becoming teenage "confession" magazines, majoring in romance and sex, while others specialize in cars, careers, or culture. Your generation is the first in America to have so much teen information at your disposal.

The next step isn't difficult to understand: "teenage" gradually became a separate way of life. Instead of being a stumbling step from childhood into adulthood, it became a culture of its own, with a special language, set of values, program of activities, and philosophy of life. You and your teen friends today have a world all your own, with "teenage" substitutes for just about everything in adult life. You have your own status system and status symbols. You have your own social merry-go-round. You are the victims of a social change that perhaps nobody could have controlled, but that everybody had better understand.

Let me go one step further: Mr. Manufacturer and Mr. Advertiser are now working on the subteens, preparing them to be "good" teenage customers! Not long ago I visited a large toy store where the latest dolls were on display. Not baby dolls, mind you, nor bride dolls, nor dutiful homemakers. *Teenage dolls!*—complete with their own wardrobe (at a price), telephone ("Every teenage girl deserves her own phone!"), TV set, sports equipment, cars, and dates. (You pay more for the boy teenager, but the girl doll won't be happy without him.) Millions of dolls of one series have been sold in the last few years, along with her 60-plus wardrobe items that add over $100 to the original purchase price!

With millions of American subteens "playing teenager" with their dolls, it won't be long before they'll all believe that their teen years are made up of nothing but dates, telephones, parties, clothes, and cars. But won't the American manufacturers be happy!

I'm not on an antitoy crusade. I'm just trying to explain the problem you have to face in your teen years. You live in a society that has twisted the meaning of the word *teenager*, a society that consciously or unconsciously is trying to make you an artificial adult. Advertisers know they can play on your emotions and peddle their goods. They gain a profit, you lose a precious personality. You find yourself following the crowd in everything, living for material things instead of real values, and wasting your teen years "playing adult." Then when you graduate from high school and go off to college or that job, you discover that you aren't really prepared for the demands and disappointments of adult life.

It's a vicious circle: children are playing "teenager," teens are playing "adult," and when they all become adults, they discover they've already lost the game!

God wants you to live your teen years as a real teenager, but that doesn't mean you'll have to forget your friends and crawl in a cave somewhere. Rather, it means that you'll have to follow some basic principles of life, principles that were made particularly for teenagers and that have been proved a million times over. Those principles are illustrated in the lives of six Bible teens—*real teenagers*—and if you follow their examples, you'll be a real teenager, too.

Now, let's meet the first real teenager— Joseph, the teenager whose dreams came true.

3

Joseph—
Make Your
Dreams Come True!

EVERY TEENAGER KNOWS what it is to dream, to live in that magic land of tomorrow where he is always the hero and everybody "lives happily ever after." The characters in that dream may change from day to day, but Mr. Teen never changes and the theme is always the same: success.

There is certainly nothing wrong with dreams. In fact, most great discoveries and inventions started off as dreams. The mistake you can easily make is substituting dreams for honest achievement, making your dreams escapes from reality instead of blueprints for activity. Dreams *alone* never lead to success. In fact, you had better learn early that *dreams without disciplines become nightmares.* And this principle has no better illustration than Joseph, the teenage dreamer.

The Bible gives us a very full history of Joseph, starting with his seventeenth year. You can divide his exciting life into four stages: the dreamer, the worker, the prisoner, and the ruler. As you read his story you will discover that God can take a boy's dreams and turn them into reality—*if* the boy submits himself to the disciplines God sends his way.

Genesis 37: Now Jacob lived in the land where his father had sojourned, in the land of Canaan. These are the records of the generations of Jacob. Joseph, when seventeen years of age, was pasturing the flock with his brothers while he was still a youth, along with the sons of Bilhah and the sons of Zilpah, his father's wives. And Joseph brought back a bad report about them to their father. Now Israel loved Joseph more than all his sons, because he was the son of his old age; and he made him a varicolored tunic. And his brothers saw that their father loved him more than all his brothers; and so they hated him and could not speak to him on friendly terms.

Then Joseph had a dream, and when he told it to his brothers, they hated him even more. And he said to them, "Please listen to this dream which I have had; for behold, we were binding sheaves in the field, and lo, my sheaf rose up and also stood erect; and behold, your sheaves gathered around and bowed down to my sheaf." Then his brothers said to him, "Are you actually going to reign over us? Or are you really going to rule over us?" So they hated him even more for his dreams and for his words. Now he had still another dream, and related it to his brothers, and said, "Lo, I have had still another dream; and behold, the sun and the moon and eleven stars were bowing down to me." And he related it to his father and to his brothers; and his father rebuked him and said to him, "What is this dream that you have had? Shall I and your mother and your brothers actually come to bow ourselves down before you to the ground?" And his brothers were jealous of him, but his father kept the saying in mind.

Then his brothers went to pasture their father's flock in Shechem. And Israel said to Joseph, "Are not your brothers pasturing the flock in Shechem? Come, and I will send you to them." And he said to him, "I will go." Then he said to him, "Go now and see about the welfare of your brothers and the welfare of the flock; and bring word back to me." So he sent him from the valley of Hebron, and he came to Shechem. And a man found him, and behold, he was wandering in the field; and the man asked him, "What are you looking for?" And he said, "I am looking for my brothers; please tell me where they are pasturing the flock." Then the man said, "They have moved from here; for I heard them say, 'Let us go to Dothan.'" So Joseph went after his brothers and found them at Dothan.

When they saw him from a distance and before he came close to them, they plotted against him to put him to death. And they said to one another, "Here comes this dreamer! "Now then, come and let us kill him and throw him into one of the pits; and we will say, 'A wild beast devoured him.' Then let us see what will become of his dreams!" But Reuben heard this and rescued him out of their hands and said, "Let us not take his life." Reuben further said to them, "Shed no blood. Throw him into this pit that is in the wilderness, but do not lay hands on him"—that he might rescue him out of their hands, to restore him to his father. So it came about, when Joseph reached his brothers, that they stripped Joseph of his tunic, the varicolored tunic that was on him; and they took him and threw him into the pit. Now the pit was empty, without any water in it.

Then they sat down to eat a meal. And as they raised their eyes and looked, behold, a caravan of Ishmaelites was coming from Gilead, with their camels bearing aromatic gum and balm and myrrh, on their way to bring them down to Egypt. And Judah said to his brothers, "What profit is it for us to kill our brother and cover up his blood? Come and let us sell him to the Ishmaelites and not lay our hands on him; for he is our brother, our own flesh." And his brothers listened to him. Then some Midianite traders passed by, so they pulled him up and lifted Joseph out of the pit, and sold him to the Ishmaelites for twenty shekels of silver. Thus they brought Joseph into Egypt.

Now Reuben returned to the pit, and behold, Joseph was not in the pit; so he tore his garments. And he returned to his brothers and said, "The boy is not there; as for me, where am I to go?" So they took Joseph's tunic, and slaughtered a male goat, and dipped the tunic in the blood; and they sent the varicolored tunic and brought it to their father and said, "We have found this; please examine it to see whether it is your son's tunic or not." Then he examined it and said, "It is my son's tunic. A wild beast has devoured him; Joseph has surely been torn to pieces!" So Jacob tore his clothes, and put sackcloth on his loins, and mourned for his son many days. Then all his sons and all his daughters arose to comfort him, but he refused to be comforted. And he said, "Surely I will go down to Sheol in mourning for my son." So his father wept for him. Meanwhile, the Midianites sold him in Egypt to Potiphar, Pharaoh's officer, the captain of the bodyguard.

That's what happened to Joseph the dreamer. But that's not the end of the story. For the fascinating Bible record of the next three stages in his career, look up Genesis 39:1-20; 39:21—41:13; and 41:14-46.

Quite a story! Imagine what *your* life would be like if God turned *your* teen dreams into reality! Well, if those dreams of yours are in the will of God (as Joseph's were), and if you let God discipline you the way He did Joseph, then your dreams *will* come true and God will use you for His glory.

It took God thirteen years to make something out of Joseph. Frankly, my sympathies lie with Joseph's brothers when I read what kind of a person Joseph was as a teenager. He was pampered, for one thing. His old father doted on him and treated him better than the rest of the boys, and that is always a tragic thing for a teenager. Joseph did not have to work; instead, his father gave him that beautiful tailored coat that marked Joseph as a ruler, not a servant.

Joseph spent most of his time spying on his brothers! In fact, had Joseph stayed home to enjoy Jacob's pampering, he might never have become a success in life. God had some wonderful plans for Joseph; in fact, Joseph was going to rescue the people of Israel and help to make possible the coming of Christ to this world! His dreams of being a ruler would one day come true; but he would never be a success in the hands of Jacob, so God had to step in and go to work.

God used three *disciplines* to make a man out of Joseph; and He wants to use the same disciplines in your life today.

Discipline number one was *the discipline of service*. God arranged for Joseph to be sold as a slave! He lost his beautiful ruler's coat and wore instead the garments of a slave. Those hands that never knew toil were now applied to the hardest possible work.

Use your imagination as you picture Joseph, the slave.

A strong Egyptian soldier, obviously an officer, steps up to the slave trader. "I am Potiphar, an officer of Pharaoh's guard; and I need a boy to work in my house."

"Fine, fine!" replies the dealer. "I have a Hebrew lad here—not very strong, but he has possibilities."

They bargain over the price while Joseph

stands by helplessly, just beginning to realize that he is no longer a human being; he is now a piece of property!

The captain approaches Joseph. "I am your new master. I am Potiphar, captain of Pharaoh's guard. What is your name?"

Sullenly, Joseph answers, "Joseph."

Slap! The soldier's rough hand tears across Joseph's tender cheek. "Joseph *what?*"

The lad feels his burning cheek and replies, "Joseph, *sir.*"

"That's better! I can see that you don't know what it is to have respect for your elders, and chances are you don't want to work. Well, we can change that!" And giving Joseph a manly shove, he starts back home.

You can see why God had to use the discipline of *service* in Joseph's life, because only through service could He teach Joseph the important lessons he needed to learn if his dreams were to come true. For one thing, Joseph had to learn *humility,* and there is no better way to learn that vital lesson than through service. The young person who has no respect for his elders will never see his dreams come true. Peter puts it this way:

> 1 Peter 5:5-6: You younger men, likewise, be subject to your elders; and all of you, clothe yourselves with humility toward one another, for GOD IS OPPOSED TO

THE PROUD, BUT GIVES GRACE TO THE
BLE. Humble yourselves, therefore, ⌐
the mighty hand of God, that He may ⌐
you at the proper time.

God had to strip Joseph of his proud garment
and clothe him with a slave's uniform that
Joseph might learn to be "clothed with humility." The teenager who is not willing to work, to
take orders, to stoop to do the humble task, will
never experience a promotion from God in the
future.

It is not easy for today's teens to learn humility. It seems that our whole way of life exalts the
teen instead of humbles him! You have your
own stores, magazines, radio stations, TV
shows, and even your own galaxy of "teenage
stars." Teenage crime and violence have become major problems with the tragic result that
many teens who are really zeros have become
heroes. If you are not careful, you will get caught
in that "hurry-up-and-grow-up" attitude, and
you will start "living your own life" and having
no respect for your parents or other adults in
your life.

The other side of the coin is this: if you will
use your teen years to be a servant, to learn
respect and humility, when you come out at the
other end of the line, you will be ready for
adulthood. Your dreams will become realities
because you allowed God to discipline you.

There is another lesson Joseph had to learn—the lesson of *diligence*. Proverbs 12:24 puts it this way: "The hand of the diligent will rule, but the slack hand will be put to forced labor." Another wise saying from Solomon is Proverbs 22:29: "Do you see a man skilled in his work? He will stand before kings."

Diligence simply means faithfulness to do the job right. You do not find too much of this quality in young people today! "Do just enough to get by" is the prevailing attitude; and that explains why many teens never see their dreams come true. Living in a computerized age, with everything done for them, they never know what it is to work, to start a job and do it right to the very finish.

Yes, dreams without disciplines become nightmares, and the first discipline Joseph experienced was *service*. He had to learn how to work.

The second discipline was *self-control*. Joseph's master's wife tried over and over to seduce Joseph.

Every teenager knows that his body is changing, that new drives are coming to the surface, and that it is easy to fall into sexual sins. Some sex problems in your life will gradually solve themselves as you understand yourself better and become mature in your thinking. But it is easy to fall into impurity these days, with sex being promoted in almost every advertisement, on every newsstand, and in the entertainment world.

Why did God allow Joseph to be tempted? That he might develop the discipline of self-control, because *the man who cannot control himself will never be able to control others.* God had Joseph slated to be a king; but he had to prove first of all that he could rule the kingdom of his body. The reason great rulers like Samson and Saul lost their crowns was because they could not control themselves. This explains Paul's warning to Christian "athletes":

> 1 *Corinthians 9:25-27:* And everyone who competes in the games exercises self-control in all things. They then do it to receive a perishable wreath, but we an imperishable. Therefore I run in such a way, as not without aim; I box in such a way, as not beating the air; but I buffet my body and make it my slave, lest possibly, after I have preached to others, I myself should be disqualified.

How did Joseph gain victory over the temptations of the flesh? He obeyed two important rules: (1) "make no provision for the flesh in regard to its lusts" (Romans 13:14); and (2) "Flee from youthful lusts" (2 Timothy 2:22). Joseph deliberately stayed away from Potiphar's wife; and when she did tempt him, he ran the other way.

The discipline of self-control is important to your future. If you fail to learn control today, you will never know real success tomorrow. If you have serious problems in this area, be sure to go to your parents, pastor, or a Christian physician for help.

The two disciplines of service and self-control were not enough; God had to use a third discipline, *suffering,* to make a man out of this seventeen-year-old boy.

Nobody enjoys suffering, and a young person especially dislikes being held down, shackled, and confined. Yet, God permitted Joseph to remain a prisoner for over two years! He had a wonderful purpose in view, as Psalm 105:17-19 explains:

He sent a man before them, Joseph, who was sold as a slave. They afflicted his feet with fetters, he himself was laid in irons; until the time that his word came to pass. The word of the LORD tested him.

For one thing, Joseph learned *patience* as he waited there in prison, knowing all the while that he was not guilty. He also learned to trust the Word of God. Satan must have said to

Joseph, "What ever happened to those dreams? I thought God made some promises to you!"

Faith and patience—those are only two of the blessings that Joseph received in prison; but then, every young person needs to learn faith and patience if he is to see his dreams come true. "That you may not be sluggish," says Hebrews 6:12, "but imitators of those who through faith and patience inherit the promises." And James says,

> Knowing that the testing of your faith produces endurance. And let endurance have its perfect result, that you may be perfect and complete, lacking in nothing (1:3-4).

Impatience is certainly a characteristic of many teens these days. They are impatient to get out of school, and some drop out even before they are really prepared for life. They are impatient to get married, not realizing that there is a difference between *growing old* and *growing up*. The Christian teenager who has experienced the discipline of suffering knows how to trust God's Word and wait. He knows that faith and patience will make his dreams come true.

When you get right down to basics, Joseph had the potential of developing "I" trouble, and the only way God could curb it was through discipline. His worst potential "I" problem was *importance;* Joseph could have been proud, and God had to make him a servant to teach him humility. His second potential problem was *impurity;* it was the discipline of self-control that answered that need. His third potential problem was *impatience;* the discipline of suffering took care of that.

God took thirteen years to train Joseph and make his dreams come true! And you and I would not be here today had it not been for Joseph. For it was Joseph who saved the Jewish nation in time of famine; and it was through the Jewish nation that God gave us the Bible and the Savior!

God has a perfect plan for your life; but before He can use you, He must discipline you, and this discipline starts in your teen years.

Let God put His dreams into your heart. Then let Him make those dreams come true as you learn the meaning of service, self-control, and suffering.

4

David—
Your Fantastic Future

NO GENERATION IN history has ever faced the fantastic future that you and your friends face. You have greater opportunities for learning, greater tools for doing things, and, thanks to a tense world situation, a greater motivation to do something constructive. But as the motto of a large insurance company once put it, "The future belongs to those who prepare for it."

The tragedy is that too many young people are sacrificing their fantastic future for a fun-filled present. They have the idea that success is automatic in this modern world, and they little realize that the competition has never been keener or the demands greater. While they are "playing adult," some of their friends are letting God prepare them for what He is preparing for them, and they are heading toward that magic goal called "success."

Before we even define "success" or discuss the three principles that lead to it, I want you to read one of the greatest success stories in the world—the story of David, the shepherd who became king. I want you to read carefully 1 Samuel 16:1—17:54 and 2 Samuel 5:4-5.

Imagine how today's newspapers (or teen magazines) would have played up David! Manufacturers would have paid him plenty to endorse their sling shots, swords, shields, and shepherds' crooks! David didn't have too much to start with, but because he let God direct his life, he became a great success.

I've used that elusive word "success" several times, so I'd better take time to define it. Perhaps the best way to do it is to use a story that Jesus told.

Matthew 25:14-30: "For it is just like a man about to go on a journey, who called his own slaves, and entrusted his possessions to them. And to one he gave five talents, to another, two, and to another, one, each according to his own ability; and he went on his journey. Immediately the one who had received the five talents went and traded with them, and gained five more talents. In the same manner the one who had received the two talents gained two more. But he who received the one talent went away and dug in the ground, and hid his master's money.

"Now after a long time the master of those slaves came and settled accounts with them. And the one who had received the five talents came up and brought five more talents, saying, 'Master, you entrusted five talents to me; see, I have gained five more talents.'

"His master said to him, 'Well done, good and faithful slave; you were faithful with a few things, I will put you in charge of many things, enter into the joy of your master.'

"The one also who had received the two talents came up and said, 'Master, you entrusted to me two talents; see, I have gained two more talents.'

"His master said to him, 'Well done, good and faithful slave; you were faithful with a few things, I will put you in charge of many things; enter into the joy of your master.'

"And the one also who had received the one talent came up and said, 'Master, I knew you to be a hard man, reaping where you did not sow, and gathering where you scattered no seed. And I was afraid, and went away and hid your talent in the ground; see, you have what is yours.'

"But his master answered and said to him, 'You wicked, lazy slave, you knew that I reap where I did not sow, and gather where I scattered no seed. Then you ought to have put my money in the bank, and on my arrival I would have received my money back with interest. Therefore take away the talent from him, and give it to the one who has the ten talents.' For to everyone who has shall more be given and he shall have an abundance; but from the one who does not have, even what he does have shall be taken away. And cast out the worthless slave into the outer darkness; in that place there shall be weeping and gnashing of teeth."

A successful person, according to Jesus, is one who makes use of all his God-given opportunities to use his God-given abilities for the good of others and the glory of God. Read that definition again and let it become a part of you. The "talents" in this story were bars of gold or silver worth a great deal of money. We use the word "talents" when talking about playing music, drawing, and other skills; but Jesus did not mean that at all.

The men in the parable were given talents according to their abilities! In other words, the talents represent *opportunities to use abilities*. God gives us opportunities to match our abilities, and if we're faithful to use both abilities and opportunities for His glory, He considers us successful. That is why the two-talent man received the very same reward as the five-talent man: he had been just as faithful.

The story about the talents gives us the three basic principles of success—three principles that can give direction to your teen years and help you prepare for the demands of the future. All three are illustrated in the life of David.

Principle Number 1: We start as servants before God makes us rulers. "Well done, good and faithful slave; . . . I will put you in charge."

God's pattern has always been to start a man at the bottom of the ladder. Joseph, you'll recall, started as a servant in Potiphar's house before God made him a ruler over the land of Egypt. Moses spent forty years as a shepherd before God made him the great leader of Israel. Joshua was Moses' servant before he became Moses' successor. The great prophet Samuel got his start tending the furniture in the Tabernacle!

David knew what it was to start at the bottom. While his older brothers were in the public eye in Saul's army, David was taking care of some sheep. (I wonder what would have happened to David's future if he had insisted, as many teens do today, that his father let him do everything his older brothers did!) David wasn't above doing the chores at home, obeying his father, and apparently getting no reward. To put it bluntly, David knew how to serve. He realized that he would never be a success in the nation if he was a failure at home.

I like the way David was faithful to do his job, in spite of problems. When he took his sheep out to pasture that eventful day, he may have thought his brothers were getting a privilege he wasn't getting. Yet Samuel bypassed all of them and sent for David! When David took the food to his brothers at the battle, he left the sheep in the care of a friend (1 Samuel 17:20) so that his flock would not be scattered. He knew how to obey his father and respect his brothers. He was a teenage servant, not a celebrity. Even after he left his job at the palace, he went right back to taking care of sheep!

That principle applies to you today. If you resent authority and resist orders, chances are you'll never know real success when you become an adult. Most of the frustrated adults today were pampered children or teens twenty years ago. They never learned how to serve others.

Principle number 2: We start with few things before God gives us many things. Most modern teens think that life is made up of "things"—TV sets, stereos, clothes, cars, and credit cards. They forget that Jesus taught that "not even when one has an abundance does his life consist of his possessions" (Luke 12:15). God's policy is to see how faithful we are with a few things before He trusts us with many things.

Where is this more clearly seen than in David's life? He started with a few sheep when a teenager, and when an adult he received an entire nation! God saw that he was faithful to care for the few sheep, so He made him king over Israel. David killed a lion and a bear in private, so God permitted him to kill a giant in public. David sang to himself while tending the sheep, and today the whole world sings his songs as recorded in the Psalms. As a lad he delivered some food to his brothers at the front; and when an old man, he delivered millions of dollars' worth of materials to Solomon for the building of the Temple.

Let me tell you about a British youth of a century ago. He was saved when fifteen and almost immediately began to serve the Lord by passing out tracts to about seventy homes in his neighborhood. When he was sixteen he taught in a Sunday school and began to do some other speaking. At seventeen he was pastoring a small church with about forty members. That grew, and, at the age of twenty he was invited to pastor a large London church! He started with only 200 when he took the church, but before long Charles Spurgeon was preaching to the largest crowds in London! He started with a few things, and God gave him charge over many things.

You may dream of making mighty conquests

in the future, and there is nothing wrong with that. But make sure you aren't sabotaging your future by neglecting your present. The way you handle school assignments today will help determine your college career tomorrow. If you're unfaithful in the use of opportunities now, God will never trust you with bigger things later.

Principle number 3: We start with work before we experience joy.

The philosophy of many teens today is, "Have fun! Act older than you are!" Young people have the wild idea that their teen years were meant to be a circus with plenty of privileges and no responsibilities. How wrong they are! Sure, there's lots of enjoyment in being young; but fun is only one side of the picture. The other side is work. And most adults know that there's no real enjoyment in life apart from hard work.

The "fun craze" has hit just about every area of life. Check the titles of the books in your local library: *Cooking Can be Fun! Fun With Figures! Dieting Is Fun!* I once told a convention of young people that I was going to make a million dollars with a new series of textbooks: *Laughing With Latin, Mirth and Mathematics,* and *History Is Hilarious.* The attitude of many people today is this: If it isn't fun, I'm not interested.

Now, you'd better accept the fact that a real

teenager can't always have fun. He has to know what it is to work. But the wonderful part of the bargain is that the work you do today is preparing you for joy tomorrow. Today's toil is really a "postponed pleasure." It's no fun to learn algebraic equations or musical scales, but once you've learned them, you've opened the door to all kinds of enjoyment. It's no fun for a football team to exercise, diet, and practice, but these activities are actually "postponed pleasures" and investments in an enjoyable future.

David knew how to work, and he knew that employment today results in enjoyment tomorrow. You'll recall that Joseph was a failure at home because his father wouldn't let him work. Once Joseph learned how to work, God gave him all the enjoyment he could contain. And He'll do the same for you.

A real teenager, then, has *direction* in his life because he is faithful to work as a servant in a few things. He knows that when the right time comes, God will make him a ruler over many things and will give him happiness.

5

This Way to Failure

SOMETIMES WE LEARN more from failure
than from success, so I want to use another of
Christ's stories to explain some more about
those three principles of success. You perhaps
know this story well, but take time now to read
again the account of the prodigal son.

Luke 15:11-24: And He said, "A certain
man had two sons; and the younger of
them said to his father, 'Father, give me the
share of the estate that falls to me.' And he
divided his wealth between them.

"And not many days later, the younger
son gathered everything together and went
on a journey into a distant country, and
there he squandered his estate with loose
living.

"Now when he had spent everything, a

severe famine occurred in that country, and he began to be in need. And he went and attached himself to one of the citizens of that country, and he sent him into his fields to feed swine. And he was longing to fill his stomach with the pods that the swine were eating, and no one was giving anything to him.

"But when he came to his senses, he said, 'How many of my father's hired men have more than enough bread, but I am dying here with hunger! I will get up and go to my father, and will say to him, "Father, I have sinned against heaven, and in your sight; I am no longer worthy to be called your son; make me as one of your hired men."'

"And he got up and came to his father. But while he was still a long way off, his father saw him, and felt compassion for him, and ran and embraced him, and kissed him. And the son said to him, 'Father, I have sinned against heaven and in your sight; I am no longer worthy to be called your son.'

"But the father said to his slaves, 'Quickly bring out the best robe and put it on him, and put a ring on his hand and sandals on his feet; and bring the fattened calf, kill it, and let us eat and be merry; for this son of mine was dead, and has come to

life again; he was lost, and has been found.'
And they began to be merry."

If David illustrates God's principles for success, the prodigal pictures the world's principles for success. David and the prodigal stand for two opposite philosophies of life, and it's important that you know the difference.

The prodigal started with many things and ended with nothing! Like some teens today, he wanted to get all he could and enjoy it while he was young. He was indifferent to his father's pleas; he wanted "things," and he wanted them right now. "Father, give me!" is, unfortunately, the motto of many young people these days. They little realize that the person who starts off with "Give me!" ends up saying "Forgive me!"

The prodigal wanted to live, and he thought that life meant possessing things and having a lot of friends. He knew a great deal about prices but nothing about values. He thought that success was measured in dollar signs. He wanted all the things that money could buy, not knowing that the things money can buy are worthless without the things money can't buy. After all, what good is a $100,000 house if you don't have a home? Or a $10,000 wardrobe if you have a sick body? Or a $5,000 diamond ring if there is no lasting love?

You can be sure that the young person who grasps for things will never really be rich.

"Playing adult" usually includes accumulating a lot of things—teenage status symbols that never really satisfy the heart. Don't forget the rich farmer who one night heard God say, "You fool! This very night your soul is required of you; and now who will own what you have prepared?" (Luke 12:20).

The prodigal started as a ruler, and ended up a servant! What a faithful gang of friends he had—until his money ran out! The world promised him success, but he ended up with the pigs! He wanted to live "high on the hog" and ended up living lower than the hogs!

Disobedience to God's principles always leads to failure and sorrow. You may think you know some shortcut to success, but that shortcut always turns out to be the most expensive road—and detours are always rough! Be willing to wait. Be a servant today and your opportunity will come; and when it does come, you'll be prepared for it.

The prodigal started with joy and ended with sorrow. This young man was on the "fun kick" when he left home, but the fun didn't last very long. When a person lives on substitutes and those substitutes run out, nothing is left but disappointment and sorrow. He thought that real joy came from money, parties, sin, and liberty. He discovered that sin promises happiness but always delivers tragedy.

I can imagine the boy saying to his father, "It's

no fun staying at home! I'm going to leave home and have a good time in life." But when he "came to his senses," he realized that there was no place like home. The trouble wasn't in his home but in his heart.

The real teenager follows David's philosophy and is willing to let God prepare him for his fantastic future. The artificial adult, the teenager who is "playing adult," has adopted the prodigal's philosophy and wants everything right now.

Nobody has to tell you which of those two philosophies is the better.

Which one have you chosen?

6

Daniel—
Transformer or
Conformer?

THE TWO REAL teenagers we've met so far have helped you understand, I hope, the *disciplines* and *directions* needed for your teen years. You may be saying to yourself at this point, "This is for me! I'm going to be another Joseph or David!" I'm happy for your ambitions, but I have to warn you: it takes more than Joseph's three disciplines and David's three directions for success to be a real teenager. You also need Daniel, that Jewish teenager refugee who eventually helped rule an empire.

You see, Daniel illustrates the *decisions* necessary to your success as a teenager.

Daniel 1:1-21: In the third year of the

reign of Jehoiakim king of Judah, Nebuchadnezzar king of Babylon came to Jerusalem and besieged it. And the Lord gave
Jehoiakim king of Judah into his hand,
along with some of the vessels of the house
of God; and he brought them to the land of
Shinar, to the house of his god, and he
brought the vessels into the treasury of his
god.

Then the king ordered Ashpenaz, the
chief of his officials, to bring in some of the
sons of Israel, including some of the royal
family and of the nobles, youths in whom
was no defect, who were good-looking,
showing intelligence in every branch of
wisdom, endowed with understanding,
and discerning knowledge, and who had
ability for serving in the king's court; and
he ordered him to teach them the literature
and language of the Chaldeans. And the
king appointed for them a daily ration from
the king's choice food and from the wine
which he drank, and appointed that they
should be educated three years, at the end
of which they were to enter the king's
personal service. Now among them from
the sons of Judah were Daniel, Hananiah,
Mishael and Azariah. Then the commander of the officials assigned new
names to them; and to Daniel he assigned
the name Belteshazzar, to Hananiah

Shadrach, to Mishael Meshach, and to Azariah Abed-nego.

But Daniel made up his mind that he would not defile himself with the king's choice food or with the wine which he drank; so he sought permission from the commander of the officials that he might not defile himself. Now God granted Daniel favor and compassion in the sight of the commander of the officials, and the commander of the officials said to Daniel, "I am afraid of my lord the king, who has appointed your food and your drink; for why should he see your faces looking more haggard than the youths who are your own age? Then you would make me forfeit my head to the king."

But Daniel said to the overseer whom the commander of the officials had appointed over Daniel, Hananiah, Mishael and Azariah, "Please test your servants for ten days, and let us be given some vegetables to eat and water to drink. Then let our appearance be observed in your presence, and the appearance of the youths who are eating the king's choice food; and deal with your servants according to what you see."

So he listened to them in this matter and tested them for ten days. And at the end of ten days their appearance seemed better and they were fatter than all the youths who had been eating the king's choice food. So the overseer continued to withhold their choice food and the wine they were to drink, and kept giving them vegetables.

And as for these four youths, God gave them knowledge and intelligence in every branch of literature and wisdom; Daniel even understood all kinds of visions and dreams. Then at the end of the days which the king had specified for presenting them, the commander of the officials presented them before Nebuchadnezzar. And the king talked with them, and out of them all not one was found like Daniel, Hananiah, Mishael and Azariah; so they entered the king's personal service. And as for every matter of wisdom and understanding about which the king consulted them, he found them ten times better than all the magicians and conjurers who were in all his realm. And Daniel continued until the first year of Cyrus the king.

The first decision Daniel had to make was whether he was going to be a *conformer* or a *transformer*. The leaders in Babylon did their best to make Daniel conform. They took him from Jerusalem to Babylon and gave him a new home, a new name, new ideas, a new diet, a new language, and even new gods! They wanted to "brainwash" him and make him one of their puppets. To be sure, had Daniel given in, he could have had status and security for years to come; but he would have missed God's great purpose for his life.

Your situation today isn't much different from Daniel's. As a Christian, your "citizenship is in heaven" (Philippians 3:20), but you're forced to live in this present world until such time as God calls you home. But this world is no friend to Christ or Christians and would like to brainwash you and force you to conform. Unfortunately, many Christian teens *do* conform and consequently miss the best God has for them.

This is a good time to make an important distinction between the conformer and transformer. A conformer is a person whose life is controlled by pressures from without; a transformer is a person whose life is controlled by power from within. Daniel had to decide (as you do) whether he was going to let Babylon change him or whether he was going to change Babylon.

Daniel could have argued his way into being a conformer. Like some teens today, he could have given several excuses (he might have called them "reasons") for going along with the pressures being applied. "Everybody else is doing it!" would have sounded like a valid reason, because just about everybody else *was* doing it! It appears that Daniel and his three teenage friends were the only ones willing to stand their ground.

Of course, Daniel could have said, "The king commanded it, so I'd better obey." (Several centuries later, the apostles would say, "We must obey God rather than men," Acts 5:29.) Or, Daniel might have argued, "We can obey outwardly, but keep our true faith inwardly." They could have enlisted in a "secret service" and perhaps worked underground, except that God has no secret service, and compromise with the enemy is the first step toward defeat.

You and I have both heard (and perhaps used) those and many more excuses for conforming to the world around us and avoiding the shame and suffering that often comes to a transformer. From a human point of view, Daniel and his three friends were fools for refusing the king's offers. What a great future he had planned for them—free education, fame, security, status, and wealth! What more could a young person want?

Daniel chose to be a transformer, and I hope you'll make the same decision. In order to understand what it means to be a transformer, we must discover the pressures around you that can make you conform, and then the power God has for you to use in overcoming those pressures.

I'm sure that many times you've heard people talk about "the world" or "worldly Christians."

Or, perhaps you've read verses like these in your Bible:

> 1 John 2:15-17: Do not love the world, nor the things in the world. If any one loves the world, the love of the Father is not in him. For all that is in the world, the lust of the flesh and the lust of the eyes and the boastful pride of life, is not from the Father, but is from the world. And the world is passing away, and also its lusts; but the one who does the will of God abides forever.

You may have asked yourself, "What in the world is 'the world'?"

The Bible uses the word *world* in at least three ways. It speaks of the *material world:* "God who made the world and all things in it" (Acts 17:24); a second meaning is the *human world:* "For God so loved the world" (John 3:16); but the Bible also speaks of *an invisible system, controlled by Satan, that opposes the work of Christ*—"the world." The word *world* is used in that way in 1 John 2:15-17, Romans 12:2, John 17:16, and in many other places. When the Bible warns you, "Do not love the world!" or "Do not be conformed to this world!" it has this invisible system in mind.

Let me illustrate. Have you ever turned on your radio or TV to hear the news and heard the announcer say, "And now the news from the world of sports"? What did he mean by "the world of sports"? Did he refer to a special planet populated only by athletes, umpires, and spectators? Of course not! "The world of sports" is a phrase that includes all the people, places, events, plans, and philosophies that relate to sports. "The world of sports" includes things visible and invisible, but things real and powerful nonetheless.

All around you every single day is this invisible system that the Bible calls *the world*. As a Christian, you are *in* the physical and human world, but *not in* the world-system that is out to oppose Christ.

Perhaps a diagram will make this clear. When you came into this human world, you brought with you a body, mind, and will. All of your abilities, appetites, and achievements were wrapped up in your body, mind, and will. When you became a Christian, the Holy Spirit of God moved into your life and made your body His temple (1 Corinthians 6:19-20); so we can diagram a Christian like this:

Now, all around you is the satanic world-system that the Bible calls *the world*. Daniel had it around him in Babylon, and you have it in Chicago, Los Angeles, Grove Junction, or wherever you are. So, let's add *the world* to our diagram:

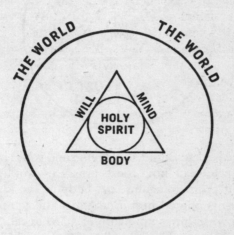

You'll remember that 1 John 2:16 identifies three "pressures" that the world exerts against you all the time, pressures that can make you conform to the world and thereby lose your testimony as a Christian. These pressures work on your body (the lust, or appetite, of the flesh), your mind (the appetite of the eyes), and your will (the pride of life). Let's add those pressures to our diagram:

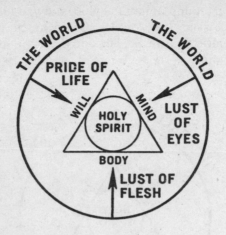

Go back to Daniel in Babylon and you'll have some idea of how these pressures work. He faced pressure against his body as the king's servants offered him a new diet and tempted him with things unlawful for a Jew to eat. The new ideas and "wisdom" that they taught him exerted pressure against his mind—not unlike modern brainwashing. And the wonderful offers of money and position worked on his will and would have conquered him. Had Daniel given in to these subtle pressures, he would have become a conformer, lost his testimony and power, and never gone down in history as a real teenager.

But he didn't give in! Daniel knew the secret of being a transformer, and he used the divine power within him to overcome the pressures without. What is that secret?

> Romans 12:1-2: I urge you therefore, brethren, by the mercies of God, to present your bodies a living and holy sacrifice, acceptable to God, which is your spiritual service of worship. And do not be conformed to this world, but be transformed by the renewing of your mind, that you may prove what the will of God is, that which is good and acceptable and perfect.

Note those two important words, *conformed* and *transformed*. Paul tells us here that any Christian can be a transformer by surrendering himself to God—body, mind, and will. Observe that truth in Romans 12:1-2 (italics added):

> "present your *bodies* a living and holy sacrifice"
>
> "the renewing of your *mind*."
>
> "prove . . . *the will* of God . . . which is good and acceptable and perfect."

That's the meaning of dedication: daily surrendering of body, mind, and will to God for Him to control and use.

Here's how it works. You wake up in the morning and the very first thing you do is yield your body, mind, and will to God. This is an act of faith, a "spiritual sacrifice" similar to the burnt offering the Jewish priests placed on the altar early each morning. Then you get up and open your Bible, allowing the Word of God to renew your mind. That means reading the Word, understanding it, and making it a part of your life.

The next step is prayer, and here you present to God your praise and petitions with a yielded will. "Not my will, but Yours be done!" When you have done this, you are a dedicated teenager and the indwelling Holy Spirit is in control. (If this is merely a routine, of course, there is no dedication. It has to come from the heart.)

No sooner do you step out of your room than the world starts putting pressure on you. Perhaps it exerts pressure against your body, trying to get you to live for your body or use your body as the people of the world do. When you sense that pressure at work, simply say, "Father, take over my body! It's yielded to Your control!" The Spirit on the inside counteracts the pressure on the outside—and you get the victory!

Perhaps the pressure is exerted against your mind, and you're tempted to think the way the world thinks—"Go ahead and cheat on the exam! You'll get away with it. Everybody does." When you turn your mind over to God by faith, the power on the inside (the Holy Spirit) counteracts the pressure on the outside, and you overcome that temptation.

Perhaps you're walking down the corridor at school and somebody races by, knocking you into the wall and scattering your books all over the place. That proud will of yours (and we all have one!) immediately reacts, and the pressure from the world goes to work, tempting you to lose your temper and tell somebody what you think. Instead, you ask the Spirit to take over. His power from within counteracts that pressure from without, and you smile and get the victory—and give a better testimony.

That is the simple secret of being a transformer instead of a conformer. Because Daniel surrendered body, mind, and will to God, and spent time daily in the Word of God and prayer (see Daniel 6:1-11 and 9:2), he was able to live a godly life in a very ungodly nation. Because he fixed his heart on God and not on the world, God honored him and made him a real success in every way (see Daniel 1:8-20).

There's one more matter I want to discuss before we leave Daniel and move into the New Testament to meet another real teenager, and that's the subject of *worldliness*. What is worldliness? How can you tell when those pressures are at work in your life? How can a Christian teenager tell right from wrong when so many Christians disagree on these matters? I'll take these questions up in the next chapter, but I'd suggest you visit Daniel again and review this chapter carefully.

7

How Can a Teenager Know Right From Wrong?

HE HAD A determined look on his face, and he was heading right for me! I had just finished speaking to a youth conference, and apparently something I had said had aroused either his interest or his anger.

"This business about conforming to the world is all well and good," he exploded, without even introducing himself, "but the world *I* live in isn't black and white. It's various shades of gray, and sometimes I don't really know what's right and what's wrong!"

"That's interesting," I replied, "because people in biblical times faced the same problem. Have you ever read Paul's first letter to the Christians at Corinth?"

"A little," he answered. "But those people didn't know anything about TV programs or movies or any of the other things that bother me and my Christian friends." Then he asked the question I had heard scores of teens ask across the country: "Just how can a Christian teenager know right from wrong?"

We sat down with our Bibles, opened to 1 Corinthians, and discovered the answer to that question. Put yourself in that young man's place and let me show you how the Bible solves this typical teen problem.

To begin with, the Bible deals with *principles,* not rules and regulations. Of course, there are specific rules and warnings in the Bible; but when it comes to the area of questionable things, the Bible lays down principles instead.

A principle is something that applies and works regardless of the time or situation, while a specific rule usually applies to a specific situation. Some sins, of course, can be named specifically: it's *always* wrong to lie, steal, lose your temper, and so forth. You will find those sins in *every* culture and civilization. But matters like TV viewing, movies, and the use of drugs are relatively modern, and the Bible doesn't mention them. Instead, God gives us basic principles, or tests, that apply just as effectively today as they did in Corinth or Rome twenty centuries ago.

If you had been a Christian teenager in

Corinth, for example, you would have faced the problem of food being offered to idols (1 Corinthians 8). We all know that an idol is not a real god, and that food dedicated to an idol is not contaminated. But some Christians at Corinth were offended when their Christian friends ate meat that had been offered to idols when it was served to them in their friends' houses. (In fact, the cheapest meat in town came from the temple sacrifices!)

Instead of saying, "Thou shalt not!" the apostle Paul gave four spiritual principles (or tests) for the believers to apply to their own lives. These four principles answer the question, "How can a Christian know right from wrong?"

1. *Will this lead to freedom, or slavery?* Read 1 Corinthians 6:12:

> All things are lawful for me, but not all things are profitable. All things are lawful for me, but I will not be mastered by anything.

The real issue, then, is not whether a thing is lawful or even approved; the issue is, *Will it make a slave out of me?* Anything that gets control over a Christian is wrong, even if others think it is right.

Take sports, for example. I have seen wonderful Christian fellows go downhill spiritually after getting involved with school athletics. Not that playing football or baseball is a sin. In fact, participation in school sports can be a real testimony—provided the Lord comes first. But when a Christian teenager's mind is so filled with winning the game that he has no thought for the Bible, prayer, witnessing, church, or other spiritual matters, he has become a slave—and that is sin.

The same principle applies to dating: if a fellow or girl becomes so important that Christ loses His place of preeminence, even Christians dating other Christians and going to Christian places can be wrong.

2. *Is this thing making me a stumbling block or a stepping-stone?* Read 1 Corinthians 8:9:

> But take care lest this liberty of yours somehow become a stumbling block to the weak.

"You and I both know," writes Paul, in other words, "that eating dedicated meat in a heathen temple is not going to make you spiritually weak. But suppose a weaker Christian sees you there, and his own conscience is offended? He will use you as an excuse to do things that used to bother him, and if he ends up in sin, you are to blame!"

The real issue is not what these questionable practices will do to *you* personally, but *what they will do to those who watch you.* After all, you are the best Christian somebody knows! It is far better to sacrifice the questionable thing and be the best example possible than to risk the danger of making some other teenager stumble into sin.

3. *Will it build me up or tear me down?* Read 1 Corinthians 10:23 (the word "edify" in this verse means "to build up"):

> All things are lawful, but not all things are profitable. All things are lawful, but not all things edify.

Life is too short to be tearing yourself down physically, mentally, emotionally, or spiritually! You have only one body; take care of it! Your Uncle Pete may be able to read certain magazines, but if you read them, they would tear you down. If you detect *anything* in your life—even a "good" thing—that dulls your spiritual appetite or makes it easy to sin, get rid of it in a hurry.

Now, that doesn't mean that you should experiment with sin. You don't have to rob a bank or cheat on an exam to discover that stealing will tear you down. You don't have to walk in the back door of the local tavern to know that alcohol is a destroyer.

These practices are pretty clearly covered in the Bible as well as in the experience of mature people down through the years. But when it comes to the questionable things that even some Christians disagree on, you'll have to test them for yourself—honestly and prayerfully—to see whether they build you up or tear you down.

4. *Will this simply please me, or will it glorify God?* Read 1 Corinthians 10:31:

Whether, then, you eat or drink or whatever you do, do all to the glory of God.

As a Christian, your privilege—and responsibility—is to use your body to *glorify* God and to *magnify* God. "Therefore glorify God in your body," commands 1 Corinthians 6:20; and Paul says in Philippians 1:20 that he wants Christ to be magnified, or exalted, in his body, "whether by life or by death." If you practice something that glorifies you or magnifies you in the eyes of your friends, but minimizes (or even disgraces) your Savior, that practice is wrong. In fact, it's just plain selfish!

Those are four tests you can use every day to decide what is right and wrong in this area of questionable things. The only requirement is that you be perfectly honest in your dealings with God. "Let each man be fully convinced in his own mind" (Romans 14:5). It would pay for you to read all of Romans 14 because it deals in detail with this problem.

This much is certain: the Christian teenager who honestly follows these principles, and who is anxious to please Christ in everything, will find himself walking in the sunlight of God's best instead of the shadows of compromise.

8

Mary—
You Can Be a Miracle!

"WHY IN THE world did you do it?" the juvenile court judge asked four teenagers accused of breaking into a garage and beating up an old watchman—all for $1.76!

"There was nothin' else to do," the ringleader answered. "We just got bored and wanted something to do. That's all."

Boredom—nothing to do—is a real problem with many young people. (Not that schoolwork and home responsibilities aren't enough to keep you busy!) Life can become (as one girl explained to me) "just plain ordinary." And when life gets ordinary, you start looking for excitement—cars, dates, crowds, entertainment, and (too often) sin.

Life could have been ordinary for Mary, the

teenage girl God chose to become the mother of Jesus. (That's right—I said *teenage* girl. Jewish girls married in their teens in those days, and most authorities I've consulted agree that Mary was probably about fifteen or sixteen when she gave birth to Jesus.) She lived in the village of Nazareth, not the big city of Jerusalem.

Nazareth was located on a main highway, so she undoubtedly saw the Roman legions marching past and the merchants with their wares. But Nazareth didn't have too savory a reputation. "Can any good thing come out of Nazareth?" Nathanael asked Philip (John 1:46). Mary could have said, "Life is dull here! I'm going to Jerusalem or Rome and enjoy myself!" If she had, she would have become the prodigal daughter instead of the honored mother of Jesus!

Yet Mary was the happiest girl in Nazareth! She may not have had a large wardrobe, a bank account, or any of the scores of trinkets that many people think they cannot do without; but she was nevertheless a joyful teenager. Just read the record and notice how many times she talks about *joy*.

Luke 1:26-56: Now in the sixth month the angel Gabriel was sent from God to a city in Galilee, called Nazareth, to a virgin engaged to a man whose name was Joseph, of the descendants of David; and the virgin's name was Mary. And coming in, he said to her, "Hail, favored one! The Lord is with you." But she was greatly troubled at this statement, and kept pondering what kind of salutation this might be. And the angel said to her, "Do not be afraid, Mary; for you have found favor with God. And behold, you will conceive in your womb, and bear a son, and you shall name Him Jesus. He will be great, and will be called the Son of the Most High; and the Lord God will give Him the throne of His father David; and He will reign over the house of Jacob forever, and His kingdom will have no end."

And Mary said to the angel, "How can this be, since I am a virgin?"

And the angel answered and said to her, "The Holy Spirit will come upon you, and the power of the Most High will over-shadow you; and for that reason the holy offspring shall be called the Son of God. And behold, even your relative Elizabeth has also conceived a son in her old age; and she who was called barren is now in her sixth month. For nothing will be impossible with God."

And Mary said, "Behold, the bondslave of the Lord; be it done to me according to your word." And the angel departed from her.

Now at this time Mary arose and went with haste to the hill country, to a city of Judah, and entered the house of Zacharias and greeted Elizabeth. And it came about that when Elizabeth heard Mary's greeting, the baby leaped in her womb; and Elizabeth was filled with the Holy Spirit. And she cried out with a loud voice, and said, "Blessed among women are you, and blessed is the fruit of your womb! And how has it happened to me, that the mother of my Lord should come to me? For behold, when the sound of your greeting reached my ears, the baby leaped in my womb for joy. And blessed is she who believed that there would be a fulfillment of what had been spoken to her by the Lord."

And Mary said: "My soul exalts the Lord, and my spirit has rejoiced in God my Savior. For He has had regard for the humble state of His bondslave; for behold, from this time on all generations will count me blessed. For the Mighty One has done great things for me; and holy is His name. AND HIS MERCY IS UPON GENERATION AFTER GENERATION TOWARD THOSE WHO FEAR HIM. He has done mighty deeds with His arm; He has scattered those who were proud in the thoughts of their heart. He has brought down rulers from their thrones, and has exalted those who were humble.

HE HAS FILLED THE HUNGRY WITH GOOD THINGS; and sent away the rich empty-handed. He has given help to Israel His servant, in remembrance of His mercy, as He spoke to our fathers, to Abraham and his offspring forever." And Mary stayed with her about three months, and then returned to her home.

Exciting, isn't it! *God made Mary's life into a miracle!* Her joy wasn't simply a passing pleasure or a temporary thrill; it was something lasting and satisfying *because it was on the inside.* If you are depending on outside sources of joy, you will always be disappointed. But if you let Christ work on the inside, you will experience the miracle-joy that Mary knew—and life won't be ordinary any longer!

Mary's life held four sources of joy.

The joy of salvation. Mary was a *saved* teenager, and that is where real joy begins. The first miracle in your life must be the miracle of salvation, of putting your faith in Jesus Christ. And this is just the "beginning of miracles"!

Did Mary *need* to be saved? Of course she did! You noticed that she calls God her "Savior" in verse 47; and Dr. Luke traces her family all the way back to *Adam* (3:38). That's the whole trouble: all of us are children of Adam, and that makes us sinners. Mary wasn't saved because she was singled out to be the channel through whom Christ would come into the world. No, she was saved because she trusted God's promise.

How is *any* sinner saved? Ephesians 2:8-9 explains how:

> For by grace you have been saved through faith; and that not of yourselves, it is the gift of God; not as a result of works, that no one should boast.

By grace, through faith—it's that simple. That is the way Mary was saved. The angel said to her, "Hail, favored one." ("Grace, you who are highly graced."—author's translation). And Elizabeth said of Mary, "Blessed is she who believed." Grace and faith are the secrets of the miracle of salvation, the miracle that brings real joy.

Have you experienced this miracle? If not, why not believe God's promise and open your heart to Him? Then you will know the same joy that Mary knew: the joy of sins forgiven, the joy of being a child in God's family forever.

Mary had a second joy—*the joy of surrender.* "Behold, the bondslave of the Lord," said Mary, "be it done to me according to your word" (Luke 1:38). This is surrender, a yielding of body, mind, and will to the control of God.

This surrender was costly for Mary. After all, she was going to bear a baby and she was not yet married. Unfortunately, teenagers having illegitimate children has become almost commonplace in our time. But that does not make it right. God's plan is still that children are to result only from the sexual relationship between married couples. Mary's conception before marriage had nothing to do with Joseph; it was a miracle. She was, however, engaged to Joseph, and he willingly married her after God explained His plan to him (Matthew 1:18-25); but people would still talk, and it may be that John 8:41 reflects the attitude people had toward Christ's birth: "They said to Him, We were not born of fornication." In spite of the gossip and misunderstanding, Mary surrendered herself to the Lord for Him to use her as He planned.

There is no reason for you to be afraid of surrender. In fact, there will be no real joy in your life until you give your all to Christ. You don't find Mary complaining, do you? Of course not! You find her singing! First the sacrifice, then the song. At least that's the way you find it in 2 Chronicles 29:27: "When the burnt offering began, the song of the LORD also began." Perhaps the reason your life has been "ordinary" and joyless is because you have not yet surrendered to Christ.

Mary illustrates perfectly what a surrendered Christian does. First of all, *she lived by the Bible:* "Be it done to me according to your word" (Luke 1:38). Mary was God's "bond-slave," and that title refers to the lowliest kind of a servant. She had no will of her own; God's will, as revealed in God's Word, controlled her life. Then, *she lived to magnify, or exalt, Christ:* "My soul exalts the Lord" (v. 46), she sang.

As far as your friends are concerned, Christ is not very important: He is small in comparison to other people in their lives, and He seems so far away. You and I must be magnifiers and make Christ important and near.

The third joy in Mary's life was—*the joy of the Scriptures.* The amazing thing about her song (Luke 1:46-55) is that it is filled with quotations from the Old Testament—and Mary did not own a Bible! The common people of Jesus' day didn't have copies of the Old Testament; they *heard* it read daily at the synagogue. Mary had never gone through a Bible memory course at a youth camp, but she knew the Word of God and was able to quote it. In fact, her song contains quotations from the Law, the Prophets, and the Psalms.

The happiest teens I know are the ones who know the Word of God. You see, Satan's chief weapon is the lie; Jesus makes it very clear in John 8:44 that you can never trust the devil: "For he is a liar, and the father of lies." If Satan can get you to believe one of his lies he will have you in his hands. After all, Eve believed one of his lies (Genesis 3) and her disobedience, along with Adam's, brought ruin to the whole race! But the Christian who knows God's truth can answer the devil's lies and go on in victory. That's what Jesus did when Satan tempted Him (Luke 4:1-13); His "It is written!" defeated Satan at every turn.

The Bible is the best Book; and the best place for it is in your heart. "Thy word I have treasured in my heart, that I may not sin against Thee" (Psalm 119:11). Mary was joyful because she hid the Word in her heart and honored the Word in her life. The young person who spends time *daily* in the Word is going to recognize the devil's lies, avoid the devil's snares, and enjoy Christ's best in his life.

I said that Mary's song was really composed of many quotations from the Old Testament. She did what the psalmist had done in Psalm 119:54: "Thy statutes are my songs in the house of my pilgrimage." The Bible was not a burden to Mary; it was a blessing. Even God's laws were a joy to her! That is the real test of dedication: *Do I enjoy studying and obeying the Word of God?* If Mary could learn much of the Word without owning a Bible, how much more ought you and I to learn?

Behind the three joys we have already mentioned is the fourth joy—*the joy of the Spirit.* Don't be afraid of the Holy Spirit! If you are a Christian, the Holy Spirit lives within you and has made your body His temple (1 Corinthians

6:19). His responsibility is to make Christ real to you and to help you make Christ real to your unsaved friends. When Christ was on earth physically, He was limited by time and space. Now that He has gone back to heaven and sent the Holy Spirit as His "substitute," He can work in and through Christians all over the world. When Paul wrote in Galatians 2:20, "Christ lives in me," he was referring to the presence and power of the Spirit in his life.

It was the Holy Spirit who overshadowed Mary and made her the mother of Christ (Luke 1:35). It was the Spirit who brought the Word to her mind and gave her a song to sing. There is simply no substitute for the joy of the Spirit! Your unsaved friends may enjoy the "passing pleasures of sin" (Hebrews 11:25) as they live for their bodies and fleshly appetites; but you may enjoy the happiness of heaven through the Holy Spirit within. "Now may the God of hope fill you with all joy and peace in believing, that you may abound in hope by the power of the Holy Spirit" (Romans 15:13).

What are the evidences that the Holy Spirit is working in your life? Paul lists them in Ephesians 5:18-21:

Be filled with the Spirit, speaking to one another in psalms and hymns and spiritual songs, singing and making melody with your heart to the Lord; always giving thanks for all things in the name of our Lord Jesus Christ to God, even the Father; and be subject to one another in the fear of Christ.

The three evidences of the Spirit's control are: the believer is *joyful, thankful,* and *submissive.* Mary was all three! Now, read Colossians 3:16-17:

Let the word of Christ richly dwell within you, with all wisdom teaching and admonishing one another with psalms and hymns and spiritual songs, singing with thankfulness in your hearts to God. And whatever you do in word or deed, do all in the name of the Lord Jesus, giving thanks through Him to God the Father.

Do you see the parallel? When you are filled with the Spirit, you know it because you are joyful, thankful, and submissive. When you are filled with the Word of God, you are joyful, thankful, and submissive! *To be filled with the Spirit means to be controlled by the Word!* Because Mary knew the Word, hid it in her heart, and obeyed it, the Spirit was able to fill her and give her overflowing joy!

In the next chapter I'm going to explain further how the Holy Spirit works in your life. But now is a good time to ask yourself: "Have I let God make *me* into a miracle, or is life ordinary and boring?" Have you experienced the joy of salvation? Have you surrendered your body, mind, and will to God, for Him to use for His glory? Do you spend time with your Bible, hiding it in your heart? If so, the Spirit can fill you and transform an ordinary teenager into a living miracle!

9

The Ins and Outs of the Christian Life

DON'T SKIP THIS chapter! And don't argue that the doctrine of the Holy Spirit is for old people and not young people! You'll recall that Joseph knew the work of the Spirit in his life, and so did David. The Spirit gave Daniel amazing wisdom in Babylon, and He worked miracles in the life of Mary. If the Spirit could use those Bible teens, why can't He use you?

You ought to memorize Philippians 2:12-13:

Work out your salvation with fear and trembling; for it is God who is at work in you, both to will and to work for His good pleasure.

Of course, Paul is not saying, "Work *for* your

own salvation." Nobody can work for salvation; Christ finished that work on the cross. Salvation does not mean that Christ made the down payment and we keep up the installments by our own works! "Work out your salvation" means "Fulfill in your Christian life the purpose for which you were saved." In Ephesians 2:10, Paul says:

> For we are His workmanship, created in Christ Jesus for good works, which God prepared beforehand, that we should walk in them.

In short, God has a perfect blueprint for your life—a plan that will bring you the most happiness and Him the most glory. But that plan isn't something you and I try to "work out" on our own; it's something we work out as God works in us. That's why I've entitled this chapter "The Ins and Outs of the Christian Life." I want to get across a simple but important principle: God cannot work through you until first He works in you. He works in; we work out.

The big question at this point is: How does God work in you? The answer is: through His Holy Spirit. But that raises another question: How does the Holy Spirit work in you? That's the question I want to answer now.

The Holy Spirit never works in a vacuum; He always uses means to do His work in your life. If you were to lock yourself in your room and plead with the Spirit to make your life a miracle—all the while ignoring the *means* that He uses—you would be asking for a nervous breakdown or a satanic substitute for real spirituality. (Don't forget that the devil is an imitator, and that getting you to live on shallow emotions and false feelings is one of his most effective stratagems. When the feeling wears out, your dedication is gone, and you're discouraged.)

The Spirit wants to use three special "tools" in your life: prayer, the Bible, and suffering. Let's begin with *prayer*. Ephesians 3:16-21 makes it clear that the power of the indwelling Spirit goes to work in your life when you pray:

> that He would grant you, according to the riches of His glory, to be strengthened with power through His Spirit in the inner man; so that Christ may dwell in your hearts through faith; and that you, being rooted and grounded in love, may be able to comprehend with all the saints what is the breadth and length and height and depth, and to know the love of Christ which surpasses knowledge, that you may be filled up to all the fulness of God. Now to Him who is able to do exceeding abundantly beyond all that we ask or think, according to the power that works within us, to Him be the glory in the church and in

Christ Jesus to all generations forever and ever. Amen.

That's a long and complicated paragraph, but the main message is clear. When you pray in faith and love, the Spirit empowers the inner man and God goes to work *in* your life and *through* your life.

Have you ever noticed that the people God uses are people who pray? Even as a teenager, Daniel was a believer who practiced daily prayer, a habit he continued all his life (Daniel 6:10-11). David knew how to pray; in fact, many of the psalms are prayers he lifted to God in times of trouble and triumph. Jesus prayed and taught His disciples to pray. The Christian who prays daily is inviting the Spirit to work in his life.

Of course, praying can't be a hit-or-miss affair; it has to be a part of your life, and it must come from your heart. A hurried prayer after a hurried reading of the Bible is a mere routine, and an *empty* routine at that. Real praying has to be cultivated, just like real friendship. Rushing into God's presence, racing through a prayer list, and rushing out again is a dangerous waste of time—dangerous because it's a subtle substitute for the real thing.

Real prayer involves: (1) *adoration*, or the worship of God; (2) *appreciation*, thanking God

for His mercies; (3) *dedication*, giving yourself
to Him for whatever He wills; and (4) *supplication*, asking Him for the things you need and for
the things others need.

God not only works in your life through
prayer; He also works through *the Bible:*

1 *Thessalonians* 2:13: And for this reason we also constantly thank God that
when you received from us the Word of
God's message, you accepted it not as the
word of men, but for what it really is, the
word of God, which also performs its work
in you who believe.

There it is—*God works in you through the
Word of God.* "For the word of God is living and
active," says Hebrews 4:12; and that life and
power can be yours! Pay attention to the verbs
in that verse. Paul doesn't say that Christians
merely listened to the Word, or read it; he says
that they *received* it and *believed* it. To receive
the Word means that you say, "That's for me!"
Then you go out and obey what it says. When
your pastor or Sunday school teacher is explaining the Bible, you can either let it "go in
one ear and out the other," or you can give it
your full attention, take it into your mind and
heart, and trust the Spirit to use it to work in
your life. Really, that is a miracle, and it's

difficult to explain it! But you can certainly *experience* it if you will open your heart and mind to the Bible, believe it, and obey it.

It isn't just the *hearing* and *reading* of the Bible that the Spirit uses; He also works when you *memorize* Scripture and hide it in your heart. In Luke 8:11 Jesus compared your Bible to seed—and seed bears no fruit until it is planted and watered. When you memorize a new verse and understand what it means, and when you obey it in your life, the Spirit uses that verse to strengthen you and make you more like Christ.

The third "tool" the Spirit uses to work in your life is *suffering*. First Peter 4:12-14 puts it this way:

> Beloved, do not be surprised at the fiery ordeal among you, which comes upon you for your testing, as though some strange thing were happening to you; but to the degree that you share the sufferings of Christ, keep on rejoicing . . . because the Spirit of glory and of God rests upon you.

The Holy Spirit works in your life when you allow God to put you through uncomfortable circumstances *for Christ's sake*. That doesn't mean that the Spirit works when you suffer because of sin or because you are out of the will of God! It does mean that God uses the "furnace of suffering" to melt and purify you so that He can mold you into a Christian who will glorify Him.

This "furnace" may be ridicule or scoffing from the crowd at school; or it may be misunderstanding on the part of unsaved friends. Whatever it is, if you are "reviled for the name of Christ," you can be sure that the Spirit will be there to work in your life and give you joy in the midst of suffering.

You can see, then, how the Spirit works in you. First, He reveals a truth to you from the Word. You pray about that truth until it becomes a part of your "inner man." Then God puts you through some circumstance to test you; and if you trust in that truth from the Word, you will come through with flying colors. But, if you give up when the furnace is turned on, the Spirit will stop working, and you'll go backward in your spiritual life.

Remember how that principle operated in Joseph's life? Joseph knew from God's Word that he would one day rule over his brethren; yet there he lay in an Egyptian prison. How Satan tried his faith! But Joseph was a man of prayer, and the Spirit used the Word to build him up. And one day he was whisked out of the dungeon and placed on the throne!

This same principle also operated in David's life. As a teenager, David had been anointed king; but Saul was still on the throne. Then Saul tried to kill David! God used those difficult circumstances to work in David's life and to prepare him for the great work that lay ahead.

God wants to work *through* you, but He can't work through you until He first works *in* you. He is more concerned about what you *are* than about what you *do*, because if your Christian character is right, your service will be right. If you spend time daily with your Bible, if you have a consistent prayer life, and if you allow God to bring whatever circumstances He wishes into your life, then He will be able to work *in* and *through* you for His glory.

And your life will be a miracle!

10

Timothy—
Service With a Smile!

WHEN I GET to heaven, I want to thank the apostle Paul for at least two things. First, I want to thank him for being obedient to God and taking the gospel to Europe. If he hadn't obeyed, I might not have been saved!

Then, I want to thank him for the way he helped Timothy. Not every older Christian is interested in young people, and Timothy was probably in his teens when Paul enlisted him as a part of his missionary team. Paul didn't have the "younger generation" attitude; he believed in young Timothy and gave him every chance to grow and prove himself in the Lord's work. I wonder where our churches would be today if every adult Christian "adopted" a Timothy of his own?

As you know from reading your New Testament, Paul wrote two letters to Timothy. Paul had been arrested in Jerusalem and taken to Rome for trial. He had been released after a couple of years, and he and his associates had visited again the churches they had founded, among them the church at Ephesus (Paul had pastored there for three years). The situation at Ephesus was discouraging: false teachers had come in, and the good work Paul had done was rapidly being weakened.

Paul left young Timothy there to fight the battle while he went on to other churches; and it was from one of those churches he wrote 1 Timothy to encourage Timothy and help him in his pastoral work. Paul was then arrested again and taken to Rome. It was from his Roman prison that he wrote 2 Timothy, the last letter he ever wrote.

As you read these two very personal letters, they seem like Paul's own photograph albums, picturing his many associations with Timothy. Without much effort, you can find in those two letters at least five pictures of Timothy that illustrate what every Christian teenager ought to be.

Timothy the son. "My true child in the faith," is the way Paul addressed him (1 Timothy 1:2), because Paul had helped to win Timothy to Jesus Christ.

Timothy's mother was a Jewess, but his father

was a Gentile. We read nothing about his father's religion, but Paul does tell us that Timothy's mother and grandmother were believers: "For I am mindful of the sincere faith within you, which first dwelt in your grandmother Lois, and your mother Eunice" (2 Timothy 1:5).

Timothy, his mother, and his grandmother (and possibly his father, but we aren't sure) lived in the area around Derbe and Lystra, probably in the city of Lystra itself. Paul visited there on his first missionary journey (Acts 14:6-20) and was stoned by the people because he refused to let them worship him. It was at that time that Lois and Eunice were saved, and then young Timothy (probably at the age of seven or eight).

Immediately Paul was drawn to the boy; he claimed him as his "true child in the faith." Little did Timothy realize that his decision to follow Christ would open up for him an exciting, rewarding life that would write his name on the pages of the Bible and the pages of history! I'm sure some of his Jewish and Greek friends ridiculed his faith in Christ; but Timothy stayed true to his Lord and his friend, Paul.

Timothy the servant. But what happened to Timothy after Paul left town? For one thing, he started learning the Word of God. "And that from childhood you have known the sacred writings," Paul reminded him in 2 Timothy

3:15. Timothy identified himself with the local church and began to grow. When Paul came back to town five or six years later, he discovered that young Timothy, now a teenager, was "well spoken of by the brethren who were in Lystra and Iconium" (Acts 16:2).

This is important: *Timothy had stayed home and proved himself among his own family and friends.* He wasn't like some young people I've met who want to "turn the world upside down" three weeks after they're saved! It's wonderful to have that kind of zeal, but unless zeal is balanced with spiritual knowledge and experience, it can do more harm than good.

When Paul was advising Timothy on his pastoral duties at Ephesus, he wrote concerning church officers: "Not a new convert, lest he become conceited and fall into the condemnation incurred by the devil. . . . And let these also first be tested" (1 Timothy 3:6 and 10). You may wonder why your pastor or church officers don't brag about you and your Christian friends, or give you places of prestige or glory in the church. The reason is simple: they know you aren't ready for it. First you have to prove yourself; then God will open the doors for public service.

It doesn't take any imagination to picture our teenaged Timothy as a Christian in Lystra. He was growing spiritually and physically. I'm sure he faced the same temptations you face today, and those I faced as a teenager. *But he was learning how to serve;* he was developing a servant's mind, a concern for other people and their needs. Paul wrote of Timothy: "For I have no one else of kindred spirit who will genuinely be concerned for your welfare" (Philippians 2:20). Unlike his teenage friends, Timothy was thinking of others, not himself. Because of that, God opened a marvelous door for him.

Timothy the substitute. When Paul and Silas came to Lystra on their second journey, they needed another helper. John Mark had deserted them on their first trip (Acts 13:13) and Paul had been unwilling to take him on this second journey (Acts 15:36-41). We'll find out in heaven whether Paul was right or wrong! But he and Silas needed another helper, someone who was humble enough to do the menial jobs that would release them to preach the gospel.

They found their man at Lystra: young Timothy. He was Mark's substitute.

Paul makes it very clear that John Mark finally got straightened out and became "useful . . . for service" (2 Timothy 4:11). In fact, he wrote our gospel of Mark! But just think of what Mark missed when he turned his back on God's call and returned to Jerusalem! Though he had his times of fears and tears, Timothy "stuck it out" and remained faithful to God.

John Mark and Timothy illustrate an important truth that you'll want to learn: *Don't rush into Christian service until you're prepared for it.* I'm afraid John Mark left home unprepared. Barnabas, Paul's companion, was his uncle (Colossians 4:10). Barnabas had accompanied Paul in his mission of mercy to Jerusalem when he took relief to the famine-stricken saints (Acts 11:27-30). Mark returned with them from Jerusalem (Acts 12:25). But John Mark had not really proved himself at home, and when the going got rough, he took the easy way out. As a young man he was probably proud of his associations with the great apostle Paul—and, as we saw earlier, pride is the very thing a new believer has to watch out for.

Timothy began as a substitute, but he remained a co-laborer with Paul for nearly twenty years. You and I would know nothing about Timothy had he stayed in Lystra and refused to obey God's call. Because he gave his all to Christ, God honored him. "The one who does the will of God abides forever," promises 1 John 2:17.

Are you going to fill that place of service God has for you? Or, is somebody going to be your substitute?

Timothy the soldier. Paul was fond of using military and athletic terms. He often mentions running, wrestling, boxing, and other athletic activities; and he also uses military terms to teach spiritual truths. That's why he wrote to young Timothy: "Suffer hardship with me, as a good soldier of Christ Jesus" (2 Timothy 2:3).

Paul didn't suggest that Timothy enlist in the army of Christ; he informed him that *he already was a soldier!* The Christian life isn't a playground; it's a battleground.

Expect battles. Don't go out and deliberately start them, but expect them. "And indeed, all who desire to live godly in Christ Jesus will be persecuted" (2 Timothy 3:12). Because you belong to Christ and live for Him, the world hates you and so does Satan. You can be sure that God will give you the strength you need to face the enemies and fight the battles, so "be strong in the grace that is in Christ Jesus" (2 Timothy 2:1)!

One thing above all that is demanded of soldiers is *loyalty.* "No soldier in active service entangles himself in the affairs of everyday life, so that he may please the one who enlisted him as a soldier," says 2 Timothy 2:4. Perhaps you have heard about the Confederate soldier who did watch-repairing on the side. His unit had been stationed away from the battle for several weeks and business was booming. Then one day the order came through the camp: "Pack up! We move in one hour!" The watchmaker rushed up to his commander and cried, "But I can't go into battle! I have too many watches to finish!" His commander calmly replied, "You were called to be a soldier, not a watchmaker!" One man's entanglements almost cost an army the battle.

A loyal Christian soldier isn't going to get

entangled with the world—this would make him a traitor, because the world is Christ's enemy! Paul knew a soldier who had fallen into that trap and mentioned him in 2 Timothy 4:10: "For Demas, having loved this present world, has deserted me." Young Samson allowed himself (and his hair) to get entangled with the enemy, and he ended up a blind prisoner in the enemy dungeon. Read Judges 16 if you've forgotten.

How does a Christian soldier become entangled with the world? There are three dangerous steps:

(1) " ... *Friendship* with the world" (James 4:4).
(2) "*Love* [for] the world" (1 John 2:15).
(3) "*Conformed* to this world" (Romans 12:2).

Friends, lovers, imitators—and before the soldier knows it he has betrayed his own Captain of Salvation!

"I have fought the good fight," Paul wrote Timothy at the end of his life (2 Timothy 4:7). What better record could a Christian soldier have?

Timothy the steward. A steward is a person who guards and invests his master's wealth. His main responsibility is to be faithful and be able to give a good account to his master.

Paul was a steward of the message of the gospel. "According to the glorious gospel of the blessed God, with which I have been entrusted," he wrote in 1 Timothy 1:11. What did Paul do with that priceless treasure? He, in turn, gave it to Timothy! His last words in 1 Timothy 6:20 are, "O Timothy, guard what has been entrusted to you."

What was Timothy to do with that sacred trust? He was to pass it on to others! "And the things which you have heard from me in the presence of many witnesses, these entrust to faithful men, who will be able to teach others also" (2 Timothy 2:2). God gave the treasure to Paul; Paul entrusted it to Timothy; and Timothy was to entrust it to faithful men who, in turn, would commit it to others. That is how the Word of God came to us!

Suppose Timothy had been an unfaithful steward? Suppose he had not heeded Paul's warning in 2 Timothy 1:13-14: "Retain the standard of sound words which you have heard from me. . . . Guard, through the Holy Spirit who dwells in us, the treasure which has been entrusted to you"? What might have happened? Well, for one thing, there would have been multitudes of people who never would have heard the Word of God. The church Timothy served would have become weaker and weaker and finally passed off the scene. What a tragedy!

Put yourself in Timothy's place, not as the pastor of a church, but as a young person who has been given the treasure of the Christian faith. *What are you doing with it?* Are you guarding your faith, valuing it above everything else? Or is it just a "second-hand" faith to you? How much is your Bible worth to you? How much do you value your church, your pastor, his sermons, your Christian heritage? *You are a Christian steward, and God is depending on you to guard His spiritual treasure and pass it on to others!*

It goes without saying that Satan would like to rob you of your treasure, and he uses four devices to do it. First, he tries *false doctrine.* "But evil men and impostors will proceed from bad to worse, deceiving and being deceived," Paul warns in 2 Timothy 3:13. If he can get you to read a pamphlet by some member of a cult, or a book by some professor who denies the Word of God; or if he can introduce you to a follower of a false doctrine, he is on the way toward stealing your treasure from you. Watch out for false doctrine, no matter who presents it.

In the very next verse, Paul says, "You, however, continue in the things you have learned and become convinced of." Listen to your parents, your pastor, and your teachers as they ground you in the Word of God, and you will be a faithful steward, guarding the treasure from Satan's grasp.

The devil's second device is *false values.* "For the love of money is the root of all sorts of evil, and some by longing for it have wandered away from the faith," warns 1 Timothy 6:10. The Christian who starts living by the sign of the dollar instead of the sign of the cross is heading for trouble. Many a Christian young person has gone off to college determined to be a faithful steward and train for service, only to have a "big offer" come his way at graduation time that makes him give up his calling for an attractive salary, a home, and a position. If anything in the world becomes more important to you than the spiritual values of Christ and the Bible, you are in danger of losing the treasure.

Satan's third device is *false knowledge*. "O Timothy, guard what has been entrusted to you, avoiding worldly and empty chatter and the opposing arguments of what is falsely called "knowledge"—which some have professed and thus gone astray from the faith," warns 1 Timothy 6:20-21. Paul isn't criticizing true science, but false knowledge—the empty philosophies of the day.

How easy it is for young minds to get excited over man's wisdom and philosophy! Any knowledge that contradicts the Bible and causes you to stray from the faith is *false* knowledge, and it is poison! "Let God be found true, though every man be found a liar," writes Paul in Romans 3:4; and Psalm 119:128 reads, "Therefore I esteem right all Thy precepts concerning every thing. I hate every false way."

The devil's final device is *false living*. If he can get the Christian steward to profess one thing but practice another, he has won the battle. "Keeping faith and a good conscience," Paul writes in 1 Timothy 1:19, "which some have rejected and suffered shipwreck in regard to their faith." The fastest way to wreck your spiritual life is to violate your conscience, that inner judge God has given you to let you know when you have done something wrong.

Your conscience is a tender thing and can be easily changed from a *good* conscience into a *defiled* conscience (Titus 1:15), then a *seared* (calloused) conscience (1 Timothy 4:2) that no longer functions. All of this happens to the Christian who does not live what he professes to believe. He carries secret sins in his heart and practices them when he thinks he can get away with it. He is an unfaithful steward, and before long Satan takes the treasure away from him. He is left empty-handed, with nothing to pass on to others.

"I have kept the faith," Paul testified in his last letter from that Roman prison (2 Timothy 4:7). He was a faithful steward—as was young Timothy, his son in the faith.

"Moreover, it is required of stewards that one be found trustworthy" (1 Corinthians 4:2). I hope that includes you and me!

11

Christ—
the Perfect Teenager

A FEW CHAPTERS ago we discovered that the prodigal son was a failure and certainly not the best example for a teenager to follow—except in repentance and a willingness to come home and be forgiven. But have you ever thought of comparing Jesus Christ and the prodigal son?

For example, both of them left home. The prodigal left for selfish reasons, of course, whereas Christ left heaven because He loves us. Both of them became poor; the prodigal because he lived in sin, and Christ because He wanted to make us rich. (Read 2 Corinthians 8:9.) Both of them died. Of course, the prodigal "died" in a figurative sense (Luke 15:24), whereas Christ died literally for our sins. Both were joyfully welcomed home by their fathers.

But that's about the extent of it. You'll have an easier time *contrasting* these two sons than you will comparing them! One was a sinner, the other a Savior. One was selfishly independent; the other said, "I do always those things that please Him" (the Father).

The prodigal spent all he had on sin; Christ gave all He had to save us from sin. The prodigal led others into sin; Jesus leads people out of sin and into salvation. The prodigal started out a son and ended up a servant, while Christ came as a servant in order to make us sons of God.

What was wrong with that Jewish boy in Christ's parable? Well, for one thing, there was something mentally wrong with him. I don't mean that he had a low IQ or was unbalanced. It was just that he couldn't think straight. His mind was so filled with his own importance and his own plans that nobody could change him. To use a common phrase, he was "beside himself." That's why Luke 15:17 says, "when he came to his senses." The turning point in his life was in his mind: *he came to his senses.*

There was also something physically wrong with the boy. No, he wasn't a cripple; there is no evidence that there was even a blemish on his body. Chances are he was a handsome, popular Jewish boy with a knack for making friends. The trouble was that *he lived for his body.* Christ says that he "squandered his estate with loose living" (Luke 15:13). Instead of controlling his body, his body controlled him. "Whose god is their appetite, . . . who set their minds on earthly things," is the way Paul describes that kind of person in Philippians 3:19.

The prodigal had another problem: something was socially wrong with him. He couldn't get along with his father or his older brother. He didn't know how to make friends on the basis of his own personality; he had to throw parties and bribe people with his money. When the money ran out, the friends disappeared—and left him with the pigs!

But at the bottom of all his problems was the *spiritual* need: he was spiritually "dead" and "lost." Don't forget that a young person (or an adult, for that matter) can be physically alive but spiritually dead, without God's life within. And the prodigal son was "lost" (separated from God) long before he arrived in "the far country." "Lost" and "dead"—what a tragic condition to be in!

There are thousands of teens today who idolize people just like the prodigal son! Compare this boy with the popular TV stars or athletes who have little or no time for God, who glorify sex and exciting escapades, who win a following because of what they have, not what they are. And the people who follow them *become just like them!* That's why it's important that you fix your eyes on the best possible examples; and the perfect example for you to follow as a teenager is your Savior, Jesus Christ.

I once heard a TV commercial about a doll called "The Ideal Teen." She had clothes, a car, boyfriends and girlfriends, lots of exciting things (her own TV set, a typewriter, a radio, a boat, etc.), and she was the most popular teen on campus. Well, maybe she *was* an "ideal teen"; but she certainly *wasn't my* ideal of a teenager! If owning three closets full of clothes, a TV set, a camera, and a typewriter, and if "hypnotizing" every boy in town is an honest description of an ideal teen, there are very few "ideal teens" in this world! The tragedy is that the youngsters who play with this kind of doll may grow up thinking that the ideal teen life is made up of excitement and things.

No, if you're looking for an ideal teenager, look at Jesus Christ. Here is the record of His life at the age of twelve, just before He entered His teen years:

Luke 2:39-52: And when they had performed everything according to the Law of the Lord, they returned to Galilee, to their own city of Nazareth. And the Child continued to grow and become strong, increasing in wisdom; and the grace of God was upon Him.

And His parents used to go to Jerusalem every year at the Feast of the Passover. And when He became twelve, they went up there according to the custom of the Feast; and as they were returning, after spending the full number of days, the boy Jesus stayed behind in Jerusalem. And His parents were unaware of it, but supposed Him to be in the caravan, and went a day's journey; and they began looking for Him among their relatives and acquaintances. And when they did not find Him, they returned to Jerusalem, looking for Him. And it came about that after three days they found Him in the temple, sitting in the midst of the teachers, both listening to them, and asking them questions. And all who heard Him were amazed at His understanding and His answers. And when they saw Him, they were astonished; and His mother said to Him, "Son, why have You treated us this way? Behold, Your father and I have been anxiously looking for You."

And He said to them, "Why is it that you were looking for Me? Did you not know that I had to be in My Father's house?" And they did not understand the statement which He had made to them. And He went down with them, and came to Nazareth; and He continued in subjection to them; and His mother treasured all these things in her heart. And Jesus kept increasing in

wisdom and stature, and in favor with God
and men.

Jesus faced several problems in His teen years
that perhaps you might face; yet He won the
battles just the same. For one thing, He lived in a
difficult city, Nazareth, in the despised area
known as Galilee. The Jews in Judea despised
"Galilee of the Gentiles" and Nazareth in particular.

His earthly father, Joseph, was a poor man, a
carpenter, so Jesus had no luxuries when He
was a child and a teenager. Luke 2:24 informs us
that Joseph was too poor to bring a lamb or a
goat for a sacrifice; instead, he brought the most
inexpensive sacrifice—turtledoves and pi-
geons.

Christ's brothers and sisters didn't believe in
Him (John 7:1-5 and Mark 6:1-5); and his own
mother Mary didn't always understand Him
(Mark 3:31-35), nor did Joseph (Luke 2:50). If
you've ever complained, "Nobody in this house
understands me!" just keep in mind that Jesus
was misunderstood *all His earthly life!*

In spite of those handicaps, Jesus Christ
stands out as the ideal teenager—the perfect
teenager. "And Jesus kept increasing in wisdom
and stature, and in favor with God and man,"
says Luke 2:52. In other words, Christ was a
balanced teenager: mentally (*wisdom*), phys-

ically (*stature*), spiritually (*favor with God*), and socially (*and with man*).

Everything that the prodigal son was *not*, Jesus is! The prodigal was "out of balance" mentally, physically, socially, and spiritually; and that's why he's a poor example to follow. But when you pattern yourself after Jesus Christ, you are following the only perfect pattern God has ever given men.

Jesus grew in the four important areas of life.

Mentally. When a Jewish boy became six years of age, his mother took him to the local synagogue where he was taught the Jewish Law and the traditions of the Jewish rabbis. That was his elementary education. When he became ten years of age, the rabbi started to prepare him for his *bar mitzvah* at the age of thirteen, when he became a "son of the law" (which is what "*bar mitzvah*" means) and had an adult standing in the home and community.

Nowhere does the Bible put a premium on ignorance. In fact, one of the constant commandments in the book of Proverbs is: "Get wisdom! Hold fast to knowledge!" This includes not only an understanding of the Bible, but also an understanding of the world God made and the things that are in it. If you aren't doing your best at school, your life will get out of balance. Perhaps God didn't give you the mental equipment to be class valedictorian; but certainly He gave you sufficient tools to pass and keep up a respectable average! If you plan to major in football, keep in mind that even a quarterback has to know how to count!

The fact of the matter is, a Christian student who fails to do his best work is a poor testimony for Christ.

Physically. The word "stature" in Luke 2:52 really means "age," but it carries with it the idea of growth and development. Our Lord took care of His body and allowed nothing to harm it. As His earthly father's helper in the carpenter shop (Mark 6:3—"Is not this the carpenter?") Jesus learned how to carry burdens and develop skills. Rabbis taught that every father owed it to his son to teach him a trade. "He that knows not a trade will become a thief!"

It goes without saying that the Christian teenager needs to develop and care for his body. After all, your body is *God's temple,* according to 1 Corinthians 6:19-20; *God's tool,* according to Romans 6:13; and *God's testing ground,* according to 1 Corinthians 9:24-27. God dwells in your body; God uses your body in His service; and God tests your dedication and devotion by the way you use your body.

It's tragic the way some of today's teens abuse their bodies as they pattern their lives after the "popularity people" of their teen world. Late hours, poor diets, bad habits, impure appetites—all of these tear down the body and throw the life out of balance.

Socially. "And he went down with them, and came to Nazareth; and He continued in subjection to them" is the way Luke 2:51 describes Christ's relationship to His parents. (Of course, Joseph was His *legal* father, not His real father in the physical sense.) The first test of your social abilities is right at home! As a teenager, Jesus knew what it was to respect and honor His parents, and to obey them. "Children, obey your parents in the Lord, for this is right" (Ephesians 6:1). "Children, be obedient to your parents in all things, for this is well-pleasing to the Lord" (Colossians 3:20).

(No wonder that at the end of thirty years, when Jesus stepped into His public ministry, His Father could say from heaven: "This is My beloved Son, in whom I am well-pleased"— Matthew 3:17.)

But Jesus not only got along with His family at home; He also knew how to behave at the Temple. Luke tells of Christ's visit to the Temple at the age of twelve, when He amazed the rabbis with His knowledge of the Word. From the way the common people gravitated toward Jesus during His earthly ministry, it isn't hard to believe that, as a boy, He had many friends and neighborhood companions.

Please don't get the idea that the teenaged

Jesus walked about Nazareth in a pious way, with a halo glowing over His head! Certainly He lived a spotless life, since He is the very Son of God; but He lived a *balanced* life, and that included social fellowship with His family and friends.

Spiritually. This, of course, is the key to a balanced life. If God is where He ought to be, everything else will fall into place. "Seek first His kingdom and His righteousness; and all these things shall be added to you," promises Matthew 6:33. Naturally, Jesus did not have to be saved, since He is the perfect Son of God. But as a man, He did have to depend on His Father for guidance and strength day by day.

What a perfect example He is for your spiritual life! He was always in the synagogue on the Sabbath, even though He opposed its false teachings and practices. He depended a great deal on prayer. In fact, Luke tells us of seven specific times when Jesus prayed; and sometimes He spent all night in prayer. Think of His knowledge of the Bible! Whether Satan was tempting Him or the enemy opposing Him, He always had just the right verse to settle the matter.

If you want to live a balanced life as a Christian teenager, you must use Christ as your example. As you read the Bible—and the gospels in particular—you see Him in every circumstance of life; and you discover that following in His steps always leads to happiness and victory.

Don't stop with "following Christ" as your example, as wonderful as this is! Go one step further and let the Holy Spirit *make you like Christ!* You'll remember in our visit with Mary that we discovered that the Holy Spirit dwells within you—"Christ lives in me!" And if you follow His directions, the Spirit will transform you *from within* to be more and more like Jesus Christ.

It starts with *dedication*—the Romans 12:1-2 kind of dedication that we discovered when we met Daniel. As you *daily* surrender your body, mind, and will to Christ, the Spirit transforms you into Christ's image. In your attitudes, actions, and appetites, you will be Christlike.

Second Corinthians 3:18 gives you another secret:

> But we all, with unveiled face beholding as in a mirror the glory of the Lord, are being transformed into the same image from glory to glory, just as from the Lord, the Spirit.

A complicated verse, isn't it? It means that when the child of God spends time daily with the Word of God (here compared to a mirror), the Spirit of God reveals Christ to him and *transforms him to be like Christ!* When you look into a glass mirror, you see yourself—blemishes and all. But when you look into the Bible—God's mirror—you see Christ, and as you receive His Word into your heart, the Spirit performs that miracle of transformation, making you more and more like Him.

A spiritual Christian is always a *balanced* Christian. When you become more like Christ, you will be better physically, socially, and mentally, as well as spiritually. Of course, this doesn't mean that Christ will give you the strongest body on campus, the keenest mind, or the most friends. It does mean that He will take what you have—mentally, physically, socially, and spiritually—and develop it in a balanced way to its highest degree.

Which "son" are you following as your example: the prodigal son—or the perfect Son, Jesus Christ?

12

Don't Just
Grow Old—Grow Up!

"WHY DON'T YOU act your age?"

How many times have you heard that question?

Frankly, it's difficult for a teenager to "act his age" because being a teenager usually means jumping from one extreme to another. One day you wish you were back in grade school, protected from the problems of life. The next day you can't understand why Dad won't buy you a car of your own!

Part of the confusion and frustration of your teen years (and some teens have more than others) rests right here. In every way—physically, mentally, socially, and spiritually—you're moving from the dependence of childhood into the responsibilities and privileges of adulthood, and sometimes the bridge seems to shake. The important thing is this: don't just grow old—*grow up!* You can't help growing older; nature takes care of that. But too many people who have grown old have never grown up; they're just as childish and immature today as they were in the fifth grade.

Maturity is a word you hear a lot as a teenager. It's one of those words that isn't easy to define in a practical way. A mature person is one who has accepted himself, and who understands himself and his world, and who uses his life creatively for his own good, the good of others, and the glory of God. That's a long definition, so we'd better take it a step at a time.

A mature person *accepts himself.* He has taken a long, honest look into the mirror, and he doesn't argue with what he sees. Of course, he tries to better himself in every way possible, but he doesn't argue with his looks, his talents, or his handicaps. He doesn't live in a dream world where he's always the hero and where there are never any problems.

He also *understands himself.* A famous Greek once said, "The unexamined life is not worth living." To be sure, nobody *really* knows his own heart; but at the same time, nobody can afford *not* to try to understand what makes him "tick." If you avoid facing the brutal facts of your own personality, you will never mature. But if you try to understand your fears and frustrations, your desires and disappointments, you will be that much further along the road to maturity.

The mature person also understands *his world*, problems and all. He doesn't necessarily understand *everything* in his world, but he certainly has a good grasp of the situation. The maturing teenager tries to understand his home and what it means to his life, his school and the crowd he runs with, and his church and the things it stands for. This understanding of his teen world gives him a sense of stability: he knows who he is and where he is and why things happen the way they do. He learns to accept the occasional family disagreements because he realizes that his growing up is as much a challenge to his parents as it is to him!

Finally, the mature person is a builder; he uses his life *creatively* for his own good, the good of others, and the glory of God. He doesn't deliberately tear himself or others down, nor does he deliberately disgrace Christ. He realizes that his life is bound up with the lives of others, that "no man is an island." He directs his life and uses his talents to better himself and others and to honor his God.

That, then, is maturity—the process of growing up while you grow older. It isn't an easy process; there are always growing pains. And it isn't a simple process, because one area of your life might mature faster than another. But it's an exciting process, a lifelong adventure! If you are going to be a *real* teenager, not an artificial adult, you'll accept the privileges and responsibilities of maturity with confidence and courage.

The lives of the six Bible teens we've met in this book point the way to real success in the matter of maturity. They illustrate for you the six essentials for maturity in your teen years.

First, we met Joseph, and we learned that there can be no success without *discipline*. The undisciplined teenager will never be a mature adult. Discipline means service, self-control, and suffering. The young person who resents work (whether at home or school), who refuses to discipline his body and mind, and who steers clear of difficult circumstances, will never grow up. He'll be a pampered adult who expects everybody to live to please him—and he'll be miserable!

David taught us another lesson: there can be no success without *diligence*. There must be purpose in life or life isn't worth living. David was faithful with a few things, so God gave him many things. He was diligent as a servant, so God made him a ruler. He was faithful when it came to hard work, so God rewarded him with joy. Maturity doesn't come automatically; it's the result of diligence on your part in every area of your life. Laziness or carelessness during your teen years will show up in your adult years in one way or another.

Maturity depends not only on discipline and diligence; it also depends on *decision*, the kind of decision that Daniel displayed. You can go along with the crowd and take the so-called easy way if you want to; or you can decide to be a transformer, not a conformer. Your life is made up of decisions and the consequences of those decisions, so that, for the most part, you are weaving your own pattern. "But I find it hard to make the right decisions!" I hear you say. Of course you do; *every* Christian fights this battle.

But that's where our next Bible teen comes in; for Mary explains the secret of spiritual *dynamic*. "It is God who is at work in you, both to will and to work for His good pleasure" (Philippians 2:13). The Holy Spirit can work in your life and lift you from the ordinary to the extraordinary and make you into a miracle! When you allow the Spirit to use the Bible, prayer, and circumstances (*suffering*, in particular), then God will work *in* you and *through* you.

Timothy illustrates the fifth essential for maturity: *determination*. How many times he wanted to quit! And how many times Paul prayed for him and tried to encourage him! "Be a courageous soldier!" Paul wrote. "Guard the treasure I've given you!" Paul was going to be martyred, and he knew that Timothy would have to step in and take his place. Have you ever considered the fact that some day in the future *you* may be called on to take another Christian's place? Your godly determination today in your teen years will prepare you for that opportunity tomorrow.

Of course, maturity implies development to the full, and there must be a pattern or *design* to guide you. This perfect design is Jesus Christ. "We are to grow up in all aspects into him . . . " (Ephesians 4:15).

You can use dozens of "teenage idols" as the pattern for your life, but none of them can begin to compare with Jesus Christ. The Holy Spirit within you wants to work in you to make you like Christ. Instead of being conformed to the world (Romans 12:2), you want to be "conformed to the image of His Son" (Romans 8:29). What greater Example could you follow?

These, then, are the six essentials for maturity: discipline, diligence, decision, dynamic, determination, and design. You've seen from the lives of six Bible teenagers that those essentials *really work!* And when they work, they make you a *real* teenager!

In other words, many things in your life may seem to be handicaps. Perhaps you have physical handicaps; perhaps there are problems at home or at school. Bible teens had their problems and handicaps, too; but *God used those handicaps to make them successes instead of failures!* Because the young people in the Bible followed the basic principles that make for success and maturity, they had happy, useful lives and were able to help others (including us today!) for their good and for God's glory.

Don't just grow old—*grow up!* Be a real teenager today, and you'll become a real adult tomorrow—a Christian adult ready for the challenges and enjoyments God has prepared for you.